CINDERELLA BALL

1967 Indiana Hoosiers Run for the
ROSE BOWL

MICHAEL S. MAURER

Also by Michael S. Maurer:
Water Colors (2003)
19 Stars of Indiana—Exceptional Hoosier Women (2009)
19 Stars of Indiana—Exceptional Hoosier Men (2010)
10 Essential Principles of Entrepreneurship You Never Learned in School (2012)
50 Crossword Puzzles with Playful Narrations (2015)

Published & distributed by:
Michael S. Maurer

in association with:
IBJ Book Publishing
41 E. Washington St., Suite 200
Indianapolis, IN 46204
www.ibjbp.com

Copyright 2017 by Michael S. Maurer.
ALL RIGHTS RESERVED. No part of this book may be reproduced in any manner without the express written consent of the publisher. All inquiries should be made to Michael S. Maurer.

ISBN 978-1-939550-60-6
First Edition

Library of Congress Control Number: 2017941796

Printed in the United States of America

To Bob,

Your coverage of this story was priceless. You are quoted on the back cover. Thanks for your help at Mickey's Camp this summer. See you in August.

Michael S Maurer
6-27-17

To the members of the
1967 IU Rose Bowl team
who can no longer tell their stories:

Coach John Pont
Terry Cole
Harold Dunn
Mike Krivoshia
Bob Nichols
Jerry Grecco

CONTENTS

Foreword i
Preface iii
Acknowledgments v
Chapter 1: **Bill Orwig** 1
Chapter 2: **John Pont** 13
Chapter 3: **Harry Gonso** 31
Chapter 4: **Kentucky** 45
Chapter 5: **Kansas** 53
Chapter 6: **Illinois** 61
Chapter 7: **Iowa** 71
Chapter 8: **Michigan** 81
Chapter 9: **Arizona** 89
Chapter 10: **Wisconsin** 95
Chapter 11: **Michigan State** 103
Chapter 12: **Minnesota** 113
Chapter 13: **Purdue** 123
Chapter 14: **We're Going** 137
Chapter 15: **The Rose Bowl** 151
Epilogue 169
Interviews 175
Sources 179
Index 197
About the Author 217

FOREWORD

Mickey Maurer has written a gem that captures the rollicking, rolling ride that was the 1967 Indiana University (IU) football season. Hoosiers across the state and country would hold their breath every football Saturday and say their prayers as game after game came down to the last minute and the last few wild plays. *Cinderella Ball* beautifully portrays the 1967 IU team and why they earned the "Cardiac Kids" nickname.

There is no better person than Maurer to tell this story. He and his family have been devoted to IU, Bloomington, and the state of Indiana. The Indiana University School of Law was named after Maurer because of his incredible generosity and accomplishments. Helping to make the state of Indiana better and stronger every day has been one of the great passions of Maurer's life. His devotion to his family and tremendous business success are legendary in every part of the Hoosier state. Maurer's love of writing and his gift for storytelling come through every page of this wonderful, unlikely story of success, determination, and devotion.

The story of IU's 1967 Cinderella Rose Bowl season is a story of unexpected triumph, human heartbreak, and fierce determination. Maurer vividly illustrates that the "secret sauce" that led IU to Pasadena was the spirit of teamwork and the players' dedication to one another—the players on the 1967 team had each other's backs. Additionally, they trusted their coaches.

The Hoosier coaching staff knew they had a special bunch of young men and thought that 1967 might be a special year—and it sure was! John Pont was the head coach and leader of the team, and the other coaches took their lead from the fiery, hardworking man at the top. So did the players.

All of Indiana was wondering what kind of team IU would be in 1967, and the answer lay with the high caliber of the players on the team. It was a fun group, a tough group, and a team that didn't believe it could be beaten. They had the ability to laugh, play practical jokes, and kid each other, but they were serious on the field. The team was devoted to IU and each other, and nothing less than victory was acceptable.

Maurer's book takes us through this magical season. It chronicles unbelievable plays, incredible excitement, and heart-stopping moments. All of it leads to an invitation to the Rose Bowl that no one expected—except for the coaches and players and fans of Indiana University!

Cinderella Ball is a great tribute to an amazing team and a terrific coach. It is a great read for anyone who loves a good book, but especially for IU fans. I highly recommend *Cinderella Ball*—I could not put it down. Enjoy the fall football weekends of 1967 one more time as you become part of the history that was made by young men who knew that working together could move mountains and result in a trip to the Rose Bowl!

Senator Joe Donnelly

PREFACE

This is the story of a college football team. We will follow this team for four months, beginning with its first practice on September 1, 1967. I missed the entire show, having graduated law school in Bloomington in the spring of 1967, though I did not miss the woeful outcomes of the three preceding seasons (6-23-1). From the top of the Chrysler Building as the newest employee of a New York City law firm, I followed the 1967 team with mounting curiosity. After hearing one account after another from friends, my reply was often, "How did that happen?" That question gnawed at me for fifty years.

I did not know any of the players while on campus or the years following until 2005, when I met Harry Gonso and Ken Kaczmarek while we served in the administration of Indiana governor Mitch Daniels. Gonso was chief of staff, and Kaczmarek was the chairman of the Indiana Ports Commission. Both were competent and collegial, great guys. Through the writing of this book, my respect for them was enhanced. You will have the same experience.

Although the context is football, this story is about young men who adored their coaches and liked and respected each other and their roles. Unlike basketball, where everyone must dribble, pass, and shoot, in football, some players never touch the ball but are integral to the success of the team. The story is also about a coach who fashioned a diverse group of schoolboys into a team. Players were not only racially diverse but were also harvested from rural communities and sophisticated middle-class urban settings. The team's origins spanned the Midwest—Illinois, Ohio, and Pennsylvania—and the East Coast—Connecticut and Washington, DC. The Indiana members were recruited from the hills of Bloomington and Mitchell, the "Region" encompassing Gary and neighboring towns, and the metropolitan areas of South Bend, Muncie, and Indianapolis.

It was an age when coaches gave scant attention to concussions, traumatic injuries, and training room abuses. Football is a game of controlled violence; players sacrificed their bodies for their coaches, and teammates often crawled off the field after an injury to avoid wasting a timeout. Concussion was not seen as a serious problem. Coaches simply said, "You got your bell rung" and sent players back into battle. Readers, please understand these times and not pass harsh judgment on coaches and trainers.

I relate this story on its fiftieth anniversary. This is not a myth. These are real people— kids—and in spite of setbacks and disappointments, their story is one of elation and joy.

ACKNOWLEDGMENTS

It has been a pleasure to work with the team at IU Press. Ashley Runyon, Rachel Rosolina, and Drew Bryan are professionals with high standards. Rachel Rosolina provided many hours of assistance polishing and refining my manuscript. I appreciate her attention to detail. My publisher, Pat Keiffner, director of the book publishing division at IBJ Book Publishing, LLC, and her team of Jodi Belcher, production manager, Kristen (Hambridge) Draskovic, creative design manager, and Ashley Day, lead designer, were essential to the project. It's an honor to be among the titles published by IBJ.

A note of appreciation goes to Indiana historian James Madison for his research material and suggestions and to Julia Whitehead for her suggestions. Thank you, Clarence Doninger, Bill Orwig Jr., Carol Hackney, Steve Tuchman, Mark Deal, Morris Levy, Coach Mourouzis, and Dean Kleinschmidt for providing detail and to Tom Shine and Millard Lesch for vetting material. Thanks to Jeff Smulyan, former special correspondent for the *Indianapolis Star*, for his thoughts from the University of Southern California perspective. Helene O'Leary and Dina Kellams with Indiana University archives provided invaluable resources often used to confirm and sometimes to challenge fifty-year-old memories. Bradley Cook sourced and reproduced photographs that made the project come alive. Thanks to IU graduate student, Jessica Freemas, for the assistance in choosing photographs.

I gratefully acknowledge the valuable research, insight, observations, and cheerful support of my executive assistant Susan Roederer.

Thank you Janie Maurer, my wife, who is always my collaborator.

Finally, I owe an extraordinary debt of gratitude to the 1967 Indiana University football team, coaches, managers, and trainers whose lives I have probed in this book. A special thanks to Karl Pankratz for sharing his photographs and to Kenny Kaczmarek, Cal Snowden, Kevin Duffy, Harry Gonso, Doug Crusan, and Eric Stolberg, who made an extra effort to make sure I "got it right." Their collaboration was essential to the success of the project, and their stories are entertaining, educational, and inspirational.

CHAPTER 1
BILL ORWIG

James Wilfred ("Bill") Orwig had a problem. He stepped outside his temporary office in the Quonset hut overlooking Memorial Stadium and filled his lungs with the brisk morning air of Indiana University. He smiled with the certainty that he was treated to the most dazzling campus in the Big Ten, and at sixty he had seen them all.

His panorama was lush—rolling hills, trees, and streams, and those leaves—a slight hint of the hues soon to dominate the senses. Nobody could paint colors like that. Scores tried. Campus scenes and those in nearby Brown County State Park were splashed on the canvases of many artists, including the Hoosier Group, a small cadre of Indiana impressionist painters who dominated Indiana's art scene through the 1920s. Foremost among them was Indiana University's first artist in residence, T.C. Steele, famous for showcasing Indiana landscapes for the rest of the world.

It was easy to forget you were on the grounds of a fully functioning academic institution but for the dormitories, offices, and classrooms, which spoke of the proud heritage of the limestone quarries within minutes of where those stones were laid to rest. Students, parents, visitors—Hoosiers from across the state—enjoyed leisurely walks along the shaded paths seemingly with no time constraint and no particular destination. Orwig had a destination.

Orwig's smile broadened into a chuckle. He marveled, "What a place to work and what a perfect day for football." The new month, as if on cue, surrendered summer's intensity for a goldilocks day, clear skies in the low seventies. It was ideal for football and Orwig was a football man. Many would say Orwig was a better basketball player, and perhaps he was. A lanky 6'3", he jumped center on the University of Michigan teams and earned All-American honors in 1929. But if you asked him, he would tell you he was a football man. Orwig played end for Michigan and was chosen All–Big Ten in 1930.

The first day of practice—September 1, 1967—was his favorite day of the year. Soon Orwig would embrace the sounds of lockers slamming, cleats clacking on the cement surface, and student-athletes at high pitch—returning veterans and the sophomores impatient to begin their collegiate football careers. (Freshman were ineligible to play on the varsity according to NCAA rules.) The kids were as anxious as he was for the season to begin. First day of practice—he looked forward to it all year long, but Orwig could not shake a nagging concern.

Orwig was no ordinary observer of this scene. As athletic director of Indiana University, he was responsible for it, and now in his seventh year, he had failed to build a successful football program. Unfortunately for Orwig, football was the standard by which success in athletics was judged.

Orwig inherited a football program headed by coach Phil Dickens, a wily, folksy sort who had enjoyed success as the coach of the Wyoming Cowboys of the Skyline Conference before coming to Indiana. Dickens brought his "sidesaddle T" offense, a combination T and wing spread that presented the quarterback with the option to pass as if under a T formation or run as though in a wing setup. Dickens enjoyed only one winning season at IU and that was almost ten years before. The sidesaddle T was not working at IU and was abandoned in 1959.

Dickens "resigned" after the 1964 season. Orwig was glad to be rid of him. He replaced Dickens with John Pont, who had coached Yale in 1963 and 1964 to a record of 12-5-1. Pont was a sure bet who had played and coached at Miami of Ohio. He was even born in Canton, Ohio, the site of the Pro Football Hall of Fame. Pont counted among his mentors Woody Hayes and Ara Parseghian.

And yet while Parseghian's Notre Dame team won the national championship, Orwig's sure bet, John Pont, managed only one victory, and that was against Northwestern, a perennial second-division team. Fans of the IU football program still mooning over coach Bo McMillin's undefeated team of 1945 had come to accept losing seasons, but their support was ebbing. The assistant coaches wanted to discontinue pep rallies because they were too depressing. Only cheerleaders and second-stringers showed up. Hoosiers had low expectations. But not all of them. Not Bill Orwig. Orwig endured the home-field losses from the relative serenity of a press box seat. But he could not sit. He popped up and down and paced like a goalie in a hockey net. He seethed. Just the previous fall at the Indiana University football awards banquet after a 51-6 drubbing at the hands of Rose Bowl–bound Purdue, he told Hoosier footballers and alumni, "I am sick of losing. I was never a loser before I came to Indiana University and I intend to do something about it." An editorial in the *Indiana Daily Student* advocated patience:

> Blame Pont when he deserves it.
>
> IU football fans aren't exactly ecstatic over the team's season. Neither are we.
>
> After another year of the usual "heartbreakers," topped off with a nightmarish 51-6 loss to Purdue, hopes for next year are understandably dim—if not permanently dashed.

The old joke about IU being in the Big Ten on every day except Saturday is even making the rounds again. And one of the original founders of the Old Oaken Bucket Battle tradition now suggests we should drop the practice if the Fightin' Hoosiers continue fightin' to little avail.

Purdue Coach Jack Mollenkopf—gloating in all of the Boilermakers' rosy splendor—even went so far as to say that anyone currently living should not expect to see an Indiana team make it to Pasadena—at least not for a football game on New Year's Day.

To say the football picture at IU is bleak is like saying that Notre Dame had a fair season.

Noisy pessimists—and there are many on the IU campus—are beginning to wonder about the ability of Coach John Pont. His "Win Now" enthusiasm of a year ago has still wrought the same "Best Losing Team in the Country." Going from a 2-8 record to a 1-8-1 mark is not exactly what Noah Webster's defined as progress.

What a good number of people overlook is that John Pont has only started working with his own material—players that he and his staff recruited.

The road to victory is often a long one, with unpleasant detours, as IU fans know only too well.

But before we jump up to be among Coach Pont's critics, let's give him a chance—at least two more years. By then he will have completed his first four-year cycle—his players alone will comprise the IU team. If IU is still losing eight Saturdays out of 10, it might then be time to take a more critical view of the IU football situation. Until then let's just wait for happier days. It's hard to believe things could get any worse. And don't forget to give Coach Pont a break—no one hates to lose more than he does.

Orwig's office was adorned with pictures, plaques, and other artifacts of his life at the University of Michigan. He wore a ring with the large Michigan *M*. He never took it off. After enduring Orwig's comparison to the Michigan program more than once, some grumbled that he had not fully committed to IU. They were wrong. When Michigan contemplated the retirement of its athletic director, Fritz Crisler, Orwig had responded to quiet inquiries from his alma mater with a firm "no." He had much to accomplish at IU. Besides, his wife, Jane, loved Bloomington.

Orwig was a winner on the field and on the sidelines. As a player and a coach, Orwig had few peers. At Scott High School in Toledo he had been an all-state quadruple star with letters in football, basketball, baseball, and swimming. He loved to coach—to teach—and his record reflected his devotion, enthusiasm, and will. After graduation from Michigan, he stayed two years as a graduate assistant working with the freshmen football team and tutoring players including future US president Gerald R. Ford.

Orwig then coached basketball and football at Benton Harbor High School before returning to Toledo, where he coached Libbey High School to undefeated state football championships in 1941, 1942, and 1944.

After a short stint as athletic consultant for the Army of Occupation in Europe in 1945, Orwig returned to his hometown to coach both football and basketball and serve as athletic director at the University of Toledo. His football record was 15-4-2. He left Toledo to return to Michigan as an assistant football coach in charge of ends, coaching the 1948 national championship team and a 1950 team that won the Big Ten championship and the Rose Bowl.

In 1953, Orwig was offered head coaching appointments at the University of Pittsburgh and the University of Oregon. He sought the advice of his athletic director, Fritz, who said, "Bill, you don't want to be the head football coach. You want to be the guy who hires and fires the head football coach."

Orwig accepted the athletic director position at the University of Nebraska in 1954, where he served for seven years until enticed by Indiana University in 1961. He loved Nebraska. He said upon his departure, "The people in Nebraska and the university have been most kind to me over the past seven years. The understanding of our problems, their excellent help and their friendship have been heartwarming. . . . I leave Nebraska with the greatest admiration for its administration, staff, its teaching staff, and its increasing educational strength. . . . My thanks go to all my friends throughout the state and best wishes and hopes for the Cornhuskers for many victories in years to come."

Nebraska in the Big Seven did not come close to the accomplishments and the prestige of the Big Ten. By most accounts, the Big Ten was the premier athletic conference in the country. Orwig was certain of that. No one who knew Orwig was surprised to hear he had punched his ticket to the Big Ten. Although Indiana was a weak sister in football, the school boasted outstanding coaches, including future hall of famers Doc Counsilman in swimming and Hobie Billingsley in diving. IU basketball teams were always competitive. But football? More than fifteen years had elapsed since IU had produced a champion. Like he said, Orwig expected to do something about that.

Orwig was lured to Indiana with an offer of twenty thousand dollars a year, exceeding by five thousand dollars his salary at Nebraska. Indiana had to bid high to entice a quality athletic director. The university was ten months into a four-year NCAA probation for providing illegal financial assistance to its football players.

Coach Dickens had been censured for recruiting actions

in 1957. Big Ten commissioner Kenneth "Tug" Wilson had suspended Dickens for the 1957 season for what he termed a "consistent pattern" of excessive offers to prospects. Assistant coach Bob Hicks, who came to IU from Wyoming along with Dickens and the sidesaddle T, acted as interim head coach during that 1-8 season.

Further action was rumored as the NCAA investigated allegations that Dickens and his overzealous alumni were "purchasing" recruits. It was no surprise during spring practice in 1960 when the NCAA's eighteen-member council on rules accused Indiana of violating regulations in the recruitment of six prospective football players. Remuneration to student athletes was limited to tuition, room and board, books, and only fifteen dollars per month for incidental expenses. The NCAA cited numerous examples of IU exceeding those limitations. As a result of the investigation, IU was handed the stiffest penalty in the history of the NCAA, a four-year probation preventing every sport from entering teams or athletes in NCAA championship competitions and preventing any appearance on television. That ban extended to Doc Counsilman's swimming teams, undoubtedly the best in the nation, and some tournament-worthy basketball teams.

Dickens decried, "It's a dad-burned shame. We thought we'd done everything possible to avoid something like this. Neither I nor any member of my staff ever made any offer of any kind to any boy, or had knowledge of such an offer. This is the gospel truth." IU president Herman B Wells also denied any wrongdoing, saying,

> I cannot and do not wish to minimize the seriousness of the action that has been taken against Indiana University. It is a terrible blow and most certainly will affect our athletic program. The Athletic Department and I have spent not merely days and not only weeks but months on the matters involved. We made extensive, painstaking investigations of our own. The result was we were

unable to honestly and objectively concur in certain assumptions and conclusions on which action has been taken. On this firm basis, we presented our case with the greatest vigor and earnestness and with the concurrence of the Board of Trustees and the Faculty Committee on Athletics. We still hold to our judgments.

According to an editorial in *Sports Illustrated* issue of May 16, 1960, Indiana's biggest mistake was getting caught.

Virtually every sports-minded college these days seeks by hook or by crook to attract the most promising talent in the schoolboy athletic world to its campus. The main differences lie in whether the accent is more firmly on the hook or on the crook. Indiana's offense against the accepted standard was that its approach was blatant where that of the others is subtle, that it was bold and brassy where others are furtive and feline, that it was— in a manner of speaking—straightforward and outspoken where the fashion is to be devious and double-talking.

The article published a photograph of IU's half-completed football stadium with its naked beams and bare backside and drew an analogy between Indiana football and the fall and decline of the Colosseum in Rome. In fact, the new football stadium was completed in October of that year and seated almost fifty thousand. It was part of a broad project that Hoosiers claimed created the finest athletic plant in the nation. It was the sole bright point of a bleak span of woeful football at IU.

In the same *Sports Illustrated* issue, an article surmised that Dickens must have known what was going on and stated that Indiana wasn't very good at cheating and hiding its tracks. The article accused Indiana of having no finesse: "the recruiter would just approach the kid, tell him how much he was worth, whip out the bankroll and peel off the green. Indiana had to get caught because it didn't use any class."

The Big Ten also imposed a penalty against Indiana University, citing its findings that the practice of offering illegal financial assistance to prospective football players was widespread. It handed down a penalty of one year's probation plus forfeiture of IU's share of the league's television revenue. Commissioner Wilson said, "I have grave doubts any such practices on the scale suggested by the cases at hand could possibly have been carried on without the knowledge, and, indeed, the approval of the coaching staff."

Orwig inherited a program that kept the football coach and, in fact, extended his contract. Dickens was relieved to know he had retained his job, and in a speech to the Bloomington Kiwanis Club, he said, "I've been as nervous as a long-tailed cat in a room full of rocking chairs."

Why did Orwig dive into the cesspool of recruiting violation penalties, including NCAA and Big Ten sanctions, a moribund football program headed by a presumed cheater, and a campus attitude that Indiana football was just something in the fall to pass the time until basketball started? It was a high price to pay for admission to the Big Ten fraternity, but Orwig was undaunted. He was an athlete—a competitor—and he believed and trusted President Wells when he promised his unwavering support.

Orwig had no use for Dickens and his propensity to cut recruiting corners. None. Zero. Orwig did not bring his business home, but that subject was often dinner-table conversation. In his first speech one month after arriving on campus, he told the Bloomington Varsity Club, "No strong athletic program has been built on fraud. We'll never have a part of that as long as I am the director at Indiana University. I know there have been mistakes made here and I think they have been honest ones. These are mistakes to be corrected." Orwig spoke individually with a number of boosters, those who financed Dickens's recruiting program. He told them their period of "undue influence" was over. He said to one infamous booster, a Bloomington physician, "You are done. If you want to buy tickets to a game, that's fine, go sit in the stands. Your influence is over. Period." Those mistakes were rectified, and Indiana earned the right to shed its probationary status. The Big Ten restored good standing in 1961, and the NCAA probation was erased in 1964. So was Dickens. He would never coach a football team at the college level again.

The athletic department was the only stain at IU, a distinguished institution thriving under the leadership of Wells, an icon who was known as a masterful recruiter, a visionary, and a president for the ages. Like most in the IU family, Orwig held Wells in the highest esteem. Their friendship endured.

During Orwig's interview with Wells for the athletic director position, Wells pointed out remarkable programs, discoveries, and events on the IU campus. He cited the Kinsey Institute, which was engaged in research on human sexual behavior in its biological, psychological, and sociological aspects and was making the results of such research available for use. Kinsey and his staff incorporated the institute in 1947. The following year, the institute published *Sexual Behavior in the Human Male*, a popular volume that reached number two on the *New York Times* bestseller list. *Sexual Behavior in the Human Female* followed in 1953. After its release, Herman B Wells said,

> Indiana University stands today, as it has for 15 years, firmly in support of the scientific research project that has been undertaken and is being carried out by one of its eminent biological scientists, Dr. Alfred C. Kinsey. The university believes that the human race has been able to make progress because individuals have been free to investigate all aspects of life. It further believes that only through scientific knowledge so gained can we

> find the cures for the emotional and social maladies in our society.... I agree in saying that we have large faith in the values of knowledge, little faith in ignorance.

Wells confided to Orwig with a grin that Kinsey's books were widely praised and widely damned.

Wells said somewhat in jest that millions of teeth owe their good health to the development at IU of Crest toothpaste in the mid-1950s. Drs. Joseph Charles Muhler and William H. Nebergall discovered how to add an effective stannous (tin) fluoride to a specially treated dentifrice. Before releasing his data in the *Journal of Dental Research* and the *Journal of the American Dental Association*, Muhler recruited 3,600 Bloomingtonians to brush in a controlled experimental study. The new product dubbed "Crest" cut tooth decay in half. That discovery and the royalties it earned laid the foundation for Indiana's world-renowned dental research program.

In April of 1961, shortly after Orwig arrived on campus, he learned that the campus was alive with not only seminal research but also activities including the Little 500, a bicycle race that was perhaps the only but definitely the largest of its kind. The fifty-mile sprint established in 1951 by Howdy Wilcox, executive director of the Indiana University Student Foundation, to raise funds for working students topped off a week of events that was often dubbed "The World's Greatest College Weekend."

President Wells honored his pledge to Orwig and fully supported the athletic program, but he answered to a higher calling. According to Wells, the importance of athletic success is a figment of the imagination of sportswriters and sophomoric alumni. He stated, "A member of the National Academy has more public-relations value than a championship team does, and, from a straight public-relations standpoint, I will trade two championships for a Nobel Laureate."

The Wells wish came true. Indiana University celebrated

James Watson, who earned his PhD in zoology in 1950 at IU. Watson and two others won the Nobel Prize in Physiology or Medicine in 1962 for their discoveries concerning the molecular structure of nucleic acids and its significance for information transfer in living materials.

When Wells retired in 1962, his successor, Elvis Jacob Stahr Jr., was named the twelfth president. He differed with Wells on the importance of athletics to the reputation of the university. He believed that a successful athletic program is an integral part of a great university. Stahr reiterated IU's commitment to Orwig with the enthusiasm Wells lacked. Stahr was competitive. He had served as United States secretary of the army from 1961 until he took the job as president of Indiana University. He was a fighter known at Oxford University in England as the "Colonel" while studying law on a Rhodes scholarship. After practicing law in New York for a short time, he studied Chinese at Yale University, and then served in combat in China during World War II as a United States Army lieutenant colonel. Orwig thought Stahr was one of the smartest men he had ever met.

Orwig ached to establish IU football as a perennial Big Ten powerhouse. It was essential for his athletic department to be extolled along with the other programs and institutions under the direction of his friend and employer, President Stahr, whose telephone call to John Pont closed the deal on his recruitment from Yale. His pride and the success of his tenure depended on it. Orwig liked Pont, who had produced a winning record with his ethics intact at every previous stop. But the past few seasons had shaken his confidence in Pont. Orwig was not prone to making snap decisions, but at Nebraska he had wasted no time in dismissing coaches who posted losing records, flushing three of them during his seven-year tenure. On that glorious fall day in September 1967, Bill Orwig reached a decision: unless Pont produced a winning season, it would be his last at Indiana University.

CHAPTER 2

JOHN PONT

John Pont wasn't worried. Not at all. Two hapless seasons at Indiana University, his first two, would normally have been cause for concern, but Pont knew this year would be different.

IU won two games in 1965: against Kansas State, Pont's first game as an IU coach, and Iowa. The Iowa squeaker (21-17) saved IU from the cellar. The Hawkeyes did not manage even one Big Ten win. In 1966 Pont's team performed a nearly impossible task, posting a worse record than the year before. The 1966 squad finished 1-8-1. After a season-ending humiliation at Purdue (51-6), fans clamored—even those with low expectations—"enough of John Pont." Pont knew he had the support of Bill Orwig for at least one more campaign. He felt fortunate to retain his job, given the propensity of his boss to oust coaches who did not perform, and he intended to make the most of his reprieve. He was sure that in 1967, he would achieve a winning record. It wasn't blind hope.

Pont loved the game, at all levels. He would say, "To me, the greatest sound in the world is the whistle that starts a football game in which I'm involved." He attended Miami University in Oxford, Ohio, on the GI Bill and was a starting halfback for Woody Hayes on his 1949–1951 teams, leading the nation in rushing in 1949 and setting school records for rushing and total touchdowns. At a muscular 5'7" on tiptoes, he invoked images of the television cartoon character Mighty Mouse, who vanquished opponents with his powers of flight, super strength, and invulnerability. Pont was named All-Mid-American Conference three times and All-American honorable mention twice. His uniform number (42) was retired in 1951, a tribute never before accorded a Miami athlete.

Coach John Pont preparing for the 1967 season.

After graduation, Pont served a tour of duty on a US Navy submarine followed by a year of professional football in Canada. In 1953, head coach Ara Parseghian enticed him back to Miami to coach the freshmen. Parseghian left for Northwestern University after the 1955 season, urging that Pont be named his successor. At twenty-seven, Pont was the youngest Division I college coach in the country. Pont went undefeated in the conference in 1957 and 1958, winning two Mid-American Conference Championships. After seven successful seasons, Pont was lured to Yale.

Still in his thirties, Pont brought youth, energy, and confidence to Indiana, and wisdom gleaned from Parseghian and Hayes. His hair was jet black when he arrived on campus, but by 1967 that dark hair was only a memory. Pont's eyes were as black as his hair used to be. He often focused them with an intense stare, especially when he was upset, which was often. It was rumored that Pont's fiery temperament was a byproduct of his years of playing for Hayes, a raging perfectionist. Hayes was famous not only for his Ohio State teams, which included thirteen Big Ten titles and three national championships during his twenty-eight seasons, but also his inglorious demise on national television when he punched a Clemson player who had intercepted an infrequent Ohio State pass. Hayes favored the running game. He famously quipped, "There are three things that can happen when you pass, and two of them ain't good." Pont did not adopt that philosophy. The previous season, he graduated Frank Stavroff, the most prolific passer in the Big Ten. Stavroff set a Big Ten record and five school records and was named the most valuable player on the team.

Pont had never known a losing program, and he never coached a game he didn't expect to win. Pont told everyone he could find that he would win at Indiana. He signed up for the speaking circuit and contacted Chambers of Commerce, Kiwanians, and Rotarians throughout the state. Coupled with exuberance and boundless optimism, Pont was one of the game's most analytical students. He emerged from the cocoon of Miami University when it was in the midst of earning its nickname "The Cradle of Coaches" for producing football talent that included Hall of Famers Earl Blaik and Sid Gillman in addition to Hayes and Parseghian. Pont assembled a brain trust that shared his analytical approach to coaching. He brought four of his assistants from Yale, Herb Fairfield, Jake Van Schoyck, Jay Fry, and Ernie Plank. He retained Dickens's assistant coaches Bob Hicks, Charlie McDaniel, and Howard Brown and rounded out his cadre of coaches with new hires Bob Baker and Nick Mourouzis. Orwig told Pont, "If you don't have a good staff it doesn't matter how smart or how good a football man you are. It isn't going to work."

After studying the statistics and reviewing the films of the previous two years, Pont concluded that his returning veterans, juniors and seniors, were not as lamentable as their record would suggest, but his teams lacked speed and stamina. Pont knew he needed to field a faster, leaner, and deeper team in 1967. He decreed that his backfield had to run a mile in under six minutes and his linemen under six and a half minutes in order to report for spring practice.

An analysis of his first two teams' losses revealed competitive squads despite the records they posted. The 1965 team stared perennial powerhouse Ohio State squarely in the eye before losing by one touchdown. They followed with a loss to number-one ranked Michigan State 27-13—at Michigan State—after leading the game 13-10 in the fourth quarter. They led Washington State 7-0 in the final seconds when an interception that would have ended the game was lost to an offside penalty. On the subsequent play, Washington State passed for a touchdown and made the two-point conversion after time ran out to win 8-7. IU finished the season with a close loss to rival Purdue 26-21 that featured a near comeback from a 20-0 deficit.

In 1966, although the record was worse, a game-by-game analysis demonstrated improvement. The team avenged a 1965 drubbing by Minnesota with a 7-7 tie and came tantalizingly close to a rare victory over Ohio State, losing again by one touchdown in a game Pont was desperate to win against his former coach. IU was competitive in all but two games, a shut out to powerhouse Texas 35-0 and, a week after absorbing a physical beating by All-American defensive end Bubba Smith and company of Michigan State (37-19), that humiliating loss to archrival Purdue. (It was 40-0 at halftime.) The team had limped into West Lafayette missing eight starters due to injuries, including a ruptured spleen and a blown knee. A few Hoosiers were pressed to serve on both sides of the line of scrimmage. The athletic staff and particularly Bill Orwig were enraged and vowed to remember that score for a long time. Pont told Orwig it was the worst loss he had ever endured and swore it would never happen again. Frustrations piled up in 1966, including a one-point loss to Iowa and a one-touchdown loss to Miami (Florida). Pont smiled easily and often, belying his inner tensions. He maintained his sanity and football playing condition with a fitness program that included regular handball games in the IU physical education center.

   A casual observer of the IU football scene would have concluded that with the graduation of Stavroff and the loss of promising two-year letterman Mickey Parmelee due to a broken leg suffered in an automobile accident, fans would be in for more anguish in 1967. An account by John Bansch, assistant sports editor of the *Indianapolis Star* on September 2, 1967, named five teams that could wind up on top of the Big Ten. Indiana was not among them. The Big Ten skywriters, self-proclaimed mavens of the conference athletics, rated the Hoosiers eighth place—a scant improvement over 1966. In another *Star* article that same day, Pont held his enthusiasm in check. He told reporters, "We feel we should have a break-even year and to me that is a positive step forward towards our goal at Indiana." Rubbish. Pont knew that one player, one play, one moment, could make a difference in the final score, and he could list those moments—correctable moments. He was sure his three fifth-year red shirt seniors—Bob Russell, Kevin Duffy, and Harold Mauro—and his other seniors, especially captain and two-year starting offensive tackle Doug Crusan, fullback Terry Cole, and linebackers Ken Kaczmarek, Cordell Gill, and Rick Spickard, were desperate to own a winning season before graduation.

   Pont felt that without his upperclassmen, success in 1967 would be impossible. He took inventory. Kevin Duffy was raised in Connecticut. He attended Weathersfield High School, where he began his athletic career playing football and throwing the shot put. Many eastern schools were interested in Duffy, including Army, but they required that he spend a year in prep school before attending West Point. Recruiters at Cheshire Academy, a prep school, took him and classmate John Heaton into a room at the school with a small fire pit just off the field and said this is where we meet the other team after the game and have tea. Kevin looked at his friend John and said, "Oh, no we don't." They ran to their car.

The recruiter from the University of Louisville visited Kevin, but Kevin lost interest when the recruiter bragged, "These are some of the things that we can do for you at school. You can use our boats to waterski and we can offer many additional extracurricular activities." Kevin knew what he meant. The recruiter never mentioned education. When Kevin brought it up he responded, "Oh, don't worry about that, we'll take care of that." Kevin did not visit Louisville. He visited Indiana after hearing about the university from a family friend. It was the first time he flew in an airplane. When he walked the campus paths, he knew he was home.

Doug Crusan was a rugged, 6'5" brawler from Monessen, a town of fourteen thousand in Pennsylvania steel country. In high school, Crusan played tackle on both sides of the ball, and local papers dubbed him the "Monessen Monster." He threw the shot put sixty feet, an elite distance for a high schooler. Crusan's recruitment started early. In-state schools, particularly Penn State, coveted this prize. Schoolboys dreamed of being a Nittany Lion, but Crusan spurned College Station for an appointment to West Point. The Commonwealth of Pennsylvania was baffled. It was said that if you reject Penn State, don't come back to Pennsylvania.

Similar to the Duffy situation, West Point granted a provisional acceptance: one year of prep school to polish math skills. That deficit was more a matter of curriculum than intelligence. Crusan graduated 47th in his class of 277. The price of admission was too dear. Crusan was in a hurry to play Division I football. Two neighbors, Ken DeGiacomo and Bill Malinchak, were playing for the Hoosiers and encouraged Doug to visit. After school one Friday, Doug boarded a TWA Constellation and was picked up in Indianapolis. He bunked with DeGiacomo and met many of the players and coaches. On Sunday, a winter snowstorm engulfed the Midwest and Doug was forced to board an eastbound train. By the time it reached Pittsburgh's Union Station, Doug had decided to commit to Indiana.

Terry Cole, known as "T-Bear" to his family and friends, was an Indiana boy from Mitchell in Lawrence County, just an hour south of Bloomington along a hilly Indiana county road. Cole's sister, Carol Cole Hackney, was told that the first word out of her older brother's mouth was "football." At Mitchell High School, Cole was a football All-American and was named to the all-state team for two years. He was a punishing runner who liked to fight for yards between the tackles, battles he won most of the time. People were close in Mitchell, a town of 3,500, and they were grieving. Cole's neighbor, Virgil "Gus" Grissom, one of the original group of American astronauts selected in 1959 and the first person to travel in space twice, was killed at the age of forty earlier in the year with astronauts Ed White and Roger Chaffee when an electrical short ignited pure oxygen in their spacecraft. A solid Mitchell contingent cheered for Cole in 1966, and now Cole had a special reason to give his hometown something to cheer about.

Ken Kaczmarek attended St. Joseph High School, a respectable punt from the Notre Dame campus. His team lost only four games in the three years Kaczmarek was on the varsity. Twenty players would earn scholarships from Division I colleges from those teams. A half-dozen would make the leap across the street. But not Kaczmarek. There were at least eight teammates who were deemed better college prospects than Kaczmarek. He did receive two dozen offers, but not from elite football programs. He could have attended Wyoming, Kansas

State, and Idaho State but not Michigan or Ohio State, and not Notre Dame. He narrowed his choices to five schools: Indiana, Northwestern, Purdue, Brown, and the Naval Academy. He favored the Naval Academy and its scrambling, dashing, and winning football under Heisman Trophy winner Roger Staubach. Navy ranked second in 1963 and vied for the national championship in a game against top-ranked Texas. Kaczmarek secured an appointment to Annapolis from his congressman, John Brademas, and he looked forward to football as a midshipman, until he flunked the physical. Hall of Fame quarterback Otto Graham, coach of the Merchant Marine Academy, learned the reason why and crowed, "Well, you can come here, we don't have a hay fever restriction."

Kaczmarek turned his attention to the Big Ten. His high school coach Wally Moore, who later coached Notre Dame freshmen for two decades, was his guidance counselor. "Kenny," he said, "you've got some great offers. What do you want to do once you're done playing football?" After they discussed his ambition to succeed in business, Moore suggested that Northwestern and Purdue would be the preferred schools for Kaczmarek from an educational standpoint. As an afterthought, he said, "You know if you go to Indiana you can play when you are a sophomore. You can start." Kaczmarek chose IU.

Cordell Gill grew up in Washington, DC, playing football at Saint Augustine, a parochial school. His father was a physician, and his mother was a nurse. His father stressed grades and wondered whether he could maintain a B average in a premed curriculum while playing Division I football. When he visited Indiana, coach Phil Dickens guaranteed that if he and the other recruits attended IU and went to class, they would leave with a degree. That was enough for Gill. He said, "Where do I sign?" At 5'9½", he was one of the shortest players on the team but was considered by his teammates as one of the better ballplayers. He was versatile and served Pont and his coaches in many positions over his collegiate football career.

Pont turned to a review of his 1966 recruits and liked what he saw. Those freshmen—now sophomores—were going to play key roles for him in 1967. They were guys from winning programs. Many were not recruited by major colleges, but they were all solid football players. In 1966, although freshmen were prohibited from playing with the varsity, they did play two football games with freshmen from Michigan State and Ohio State. Under Coach Brown, they defeated Ohio State. In the loss to Michigan State, like wild ponies, they were awkward and error prone, almost goofy. They lost the ball four times on fumbles and one on an interception, but they could play. Coach Brown had heaped special praise on Clarence Price, lauding the speed and agility of the 230-pound freshman from Shortridge High School in Indianapolis.

Replacing Frank Stavroff would not be a problem. Sophomore John Isenbarger from Muncie Central High School was a phenomenal football player, perhaps the only sophomore who was aptly described that way. At 6'3" he could run, pass, and kick—his best recruit. Isenbarger could have played anywhere. But to say Isenbarger was a complete football player would not adequately describe this athlete. He would probably be a starter on most Big Ten basketball teams. He ran the 100-yard dash in under ten seconds, and he could pole vault over thirteen feet.

Isenbarger spent his high school career playing for the Muncie Central Bearcats. He played football and basketball and ran track, and he excelled at all three sports. Basketball was his favorite. As a senior on a mediocre team, he jumped center, played forward on defense and brought the ball up as a point guard. It was said that there weren't many shots he didn't try. One night he went 6 for 44—they weren't falling—but that was not so important to John, who throughout his athletic career displayed not only an irrepressible thirst for competition but also a spirit that never seemed to flag. He was recruited for basketball by Adolph Rupp at University of Kentucky along with a number of Big Ten schools. Although he chose football at IU, he also played for the freshman basketball team.

In high school on offense he played only quarterback; he was never anything else nor wished to be. On the defensive side, his speed and sure hands made him a perfect safety. Schools throughout the nation recognized this extraordinary talent, including leading programs such as Notre Dame, Michigan, and Ohio State. Parseghian of Notre Dame implored the young Isenbarger, "Please come to Notre Dame." He said he needed a big quarterback. He had All-American Terry Hanratty already on campus, but unlike many of the other young kids, Isenbarger was not intimidated, not even a bit. When asked whether he felt that perhaps he couldn't play at that level, he said the thought never crossed his mind.

Michigan was desperate to land Isenbarger. He received letters from Gerald R. Ford, who was then in the House of Representatives, and from Tom Harmon. Isenbarger thought, "I'm a seventeen-year old kid from Muncie sitting in my bedroom reading a personal letter from Tom Harmon asking me to follow him to play college football at the University of Michigan. Is this a daydream?" Harmon, a fellow Hoosier, grew up in Gary. At Horace Mann High School, he earned fourteen varsity letters. He won the Indiana state championship in both the 100-yard dash and the 200-yard low hurdles. His 100-yard dash time was a half a second slower than Jessie Owens's world record. Harmon was an All-American at Michigan who won the Heisman Trophy in 1940 and was inducted into the College Football Hall of Fame in 1954. As a pilot in the United States Army Air Corps in 1943, he was the sole survivor of a crash of a bomber he piloted. Six months later while flying a Lockheed P-38 Lightning, he was shot down in a dogfight with Japanese Zeroes in China. After the war, Harmon played professional football for the Los Angeles Rams and logged the longest run from scrimmage during the 1946 NFL season. After football, he pursued a career in sports broadcasting and was the play-by-play announcer for the first televised Rose Bowl game in the late 1940s. He was married to a movie star, Elyse Knox.

Isenbarger framed the Harmon letter, but he chose Indiana.

It was close enough for his parents to see him play, he liked Pont, and, of major importance, his girlfriend was there (that relationship lasted two weeks into his freshman year).

Sophomore Jade Butcher was a hometown boy, in the parlance of IU college slang, a "stonecutter," later shortened to "cutter." The name was derived from the local tradesmen who mined the limestone deposits and cut the large layers into manageable size for delivery to the IU campus and to building projects throughout the nation. Butcher was only the second Bloomington native to play for the Hoosiers in twenty years. He was a star athlete for Bloomington High School with hands like a black hole—nothing could escape them. He played basketball and ran track, specializing in the low hurdles. Purdue recruited Butcher, but he assured his high school classmates, "There is no way a guy from Bloomington is going to go to West Lafayette to play!" Butcher's first love was defense—free safety—but any competent coach could see he had no peer at flanker.

Butcher had been recruited to IU by freshman coach Howard Brown, who was nicknamed "Gooner" by his 1945 teammates after he shaved his head as a gesture of team unity. Brown, a thick-set college lineman, left the IU team in 1943 to serve in the infantry, where he was wounded three times and earned a Purple Heart and two Oak Leaf Clusters. He returned just in time to play for Bo McMillin and earn MVP honors on the 1945 Big Ten championship team. Before beginning his coaching career, he played three years for the Detroit Lions in the NFL in six different positions. He was a reliable judge of football talent and he could spot potential. He spotted it now. Butcher and the other sophomores adored Brown as "one of the neatest guys in the world."

Eric Stolberg was a track star—a track star who preferred to play football. His high hurdle time was considered elite and still stands as a record at Cuyahoga Falls High School near Akron. At 6'2", 173 pounds he was lean and fleet, a great prospect for the US Olympic track team. But for this blond, football was a passion. Big Ten football powers Ohio State and Michigan

State offered Stolberg scholarships, track scholarships with an opportunity to play football. But Stolberg wanted to be thought of as a football player, not a track star, and he opted out. He received football scholarships from other less prominent schools, Northwestern, North Carolina, Miami of Ohio and IU. Like so many players, he fell in love with the campus and deeply respected Coach Brown and Coach Pont. Stolberg, lean and fast, was what Pont was looking for. He said to Stolberg, "I want you to come to Indiana and play for us and help us get to the Rose Bowl." Stolberg looked into Pont's coal black eyes and knew that was exactly what Pont intended to do. He told his mother he was going to the Rose Bowl. Soon after he matriculated his freshman year, Stolberg was contacted by future Hall of Fame track coach Sam Bell, who knew the fastest hurdler on campus was a football player. He pleaded with Stolberg to run the hurdles for his team. Stolberg was devoted to football and so anxious to make the team that he couldn't possibly skip spring practice and run track. He declined.

Stolberg's quest was derailed when, during preseason practice, he dislocated his shoulder. At an opening season rally before the Kentucky game, Stolberg was not announced as a starter. He slinked back to his dormitory and in the privacy of his room bawled like a baby. He swore that no matter what would happen he was going to be a starter. Stolberg kept his oath. He started every game the rest of the year in spite of dislocating his shoulder thirty times. He was forced to wear a special harness that wrapped around his bicep and attached to his shoulder pads so that his left arm could not stretch too far above his head.

As spring practice began, Pont had a revelation. Last year's most valuable player, Frank Stavroff, had been a drop-back, stay-in-the-pocket passer, a classic pro-set quarterback, who required a stalwart offensive line to provide him the time to set up and to find and secure his target, the kind of line that Doug Crusan had anchored for the past two years. Pont decided to install an I formation with the quarterback behind the center, the fullback directly behind the quarterback, and a tailback directly behind the fullback. Given the speed and wide-open style of John Isenbarger, under Pont's I formation it would take less time for plays to develop. Much less stress would be placed on the offensive line. For protection of Pont's new backfield, Crusan was a luxury, an overkill. Pont reasoned that Crusan's size, speed, and skill were more desperately needed on defense. He thought of the games in the past two years he would have won had he been able to save just one touchdown. His cadre of coaches agreed.

Captain Doug Crusan

Pont called Crusan into his office and said, "Sit down Doug, we are going to have to make a change."

Crusan took a breath and thought, "I'm going from right tackle to left tackle, maybe tight end."

Pont wasted no more time. He continued, "We're moving you to defense. On top of that you have to report back in September, thirty-three pounds lighter."

Crusan, ranked in the preseason among the best offensive tackles in the nation and a sure first-round choice of the NFL at that position, accepted Pont's offer and moved to left tackle on the defensive line, thirty-three pounds lighter.

The gaping hole at offensive right tackle needed to be filled. Pont "interviewed" a few choices. During one practice, Pont directed Bob Kirk to assist him in demonstrating a low block from a four-point stance. Traditionally, a three-point stance is employed and a high block is executed from the waist to the shoulder pads. Pont wanted Kirk to block low, from the belt to the knees. Pont asked Crusan to play the role of defensive lineman. Kirk was nervous. This was certain NFL star Doug Crusan, and last year Kirk was a walk-on. When Pont yelled "hut, hut" Kirk went straight for Crusan from the waist down and moved him out. Kirk was shocked. Pont had his right tackle. Kirk had been laboring behind Al Gage at tight end. He, the coaches, and the entire team knew Kirk's chances of ever displacing Al Gage. Kirk considered his promotion to first team offensive right tackle a turning point in his career.

Kirk's good fortune was a tribute to his effort and grit—and a late growth spurt. Like Jade Butcher, he was a hometown lad. Although Minnesota showed interest, he did not bother to visit. At the request of his father, he visited Tennessee State University, his father's alma mater, but Kirk had his heart set on IU. Although Kirk was not offered a scholarship, there was never a question. He walked on his freshman year as a 6'2½", 195-pound halfback and began to grow. Kirk was fast. He could outrun most of his teammates in the 40-yard dash. In 1966, as a sophomore, Pont didn't have a place for him in the starting lineup, but he recognized his emerging talent. Pont liked and respected him. He called the young player into his office and reached up and clapped him on the shoulder (he was now

6'3½") and said, "Bob, you have earned your scholarship." By the time Kirk graduated, he was 6'5" and 250 pounds of muscle. The offensive line lamented the loss of Crusan but respected Pont as a brilliant tactician. They welcomed Bob Kirk as Crusan's able replacement.

With Crusan and his lighter, faster colleagues on defense, Pont morphed his classic five-linemen, three-linebacker formation to a 4-4 defense—four linemen and four linebackers anchored by Kaczmarek, the sixth leading tackler in the Big Ten in 1966. The goal of a 4-4 defense is to free the linebackers. The linemen get down on all fours while the linebackers are upright with good vision of the developing play. Linemen are to keep blockers off the linebackers, and linebackers are to tackle the guy with the ball. Pont had superior personnel for the linebacker positions, and he didn't want some of his best talent on the bench. He tapped Jim Sniadecki, Brown Marks, and Kevin Duffy to join Kaczmarek. They were coached by Ernie Plank, a constant pipe smoker. Plank played football at Ohio State. After serving in the US Navy he transferred to Miami of Ohio and was captain of the 1949 team on which Pont played as a sophomore halfback. The defensive players, particularly the seniors, loved to play for Ernie. Before the first game of the season they were informed Ernie would be in the press box. They implored Pont to keep Ernie Plank on the sidelines with them. Plank smoked his pipe and commanded the defense from the sideline for the entire season.

Crusan wasn't the only footballer shedding pounds. In all, more than five hundred pounds were lost to rigid diets and rugged two-a-day and sometimes three-a-day practices, each ending with sprint drills: ten 40-yard sprints, one 30-yard sprint, one 20-yard sprint, and finally one 10-yard sprint. Nick Mourouzis coached defensive backs, kickers, and punters. He was a quarterback and cocaptain under Pont at Miami of Ohio. At these sessions he carried various motivational signs on sticks. One of them stated, "WORK HARD!" This slogan was picked up on by Nate Cunningham, who lifted everyone's spirits by calling out in the huddle:

We GOTTA WOOORRRK HARD!
We GOTTA WOOORRRK HARD!
HILL AN' GULLY-GULLY!

    Brown Marks also composed a chant. He would say, "I got that feeling" and everybody else would respond, "Oh, yeah." Marks would add, "It's time to run."
    Teammates: "Oh, yeah."
    Marks: "This is so much fun."
    Teammates: "Oh, yeah."
    Marks: "Thank God we're done."
    Teammates: "Oh, yeah."

    Chants were morale builders, not only at practice but in games as well. Everyone in the defensive huddle would reply with "HARD!" when Nate would call out his chant. After the "GULLY" the huddle would break with a loud hand clap and everyone yelling "HO!" Opponents looked strangely at this, something that normally wasn't done during a game.
    Pont doggedly pursued his goal of a leaner, faster squad. He often ran sprints with the team. Still in his thirties, he wasn't the fastest but he could keep up. No games were going to be blown in the fourth quarter this year.
    During those double sessions, Kaczmarek read an article in *Sports Illustrated* about the Florida Gators using Gatorade, a drink developed by their university researchers that helped them outlast several heavily favored teams in the hot weather. Gatorade was produced and marketed by Stokely–Van Camp in Indianapolis. Kenny showed the article to head trainer Warren Ariail and asked him if he could get Gatorade for the team. Ariail told him, "No, it's just psychological and doesn't work." Kaczmarek and Kevin Duffy told Coach Plank about Florida's research and use of Gatorade and about Ariail claiming it was just psychological. After a puff on his pipe, Plank said, "So what, even if it is only psychological why *not* use it?" He went to Ariail and within a few days the team had Gatorade.

The major social events of the spring were the Little 500, this year featuring Bob Hope, and the Cream and Crimson game, the annual intraschool scrimmage. This game marked the end of the spring football practice and put Pont's sophomores on display with the varsity for the first time. The crimson team, designated as the number one unit, started nine sophomores. The cream matched that total with nine sophomores of its own.

Isenbarger was slotted as quarterback for the crimson team. The Bansch postgame commentary in the *Star* glowed with praise of Isenbarger. He said the young man showed the poise of a seasoned veteran and that he was a key man in all three of the crimson second half touchdowns.

Bill Orwig shared his excitement with the Varsity Club, his biggest boosters, in a letter in June:

> Our team will be young with several sophomores in the starting lineup. However, there will be sufficient older hands to give it some seasoning. You are going to be excited about several of our new players. It should be a truly exciting year.

It was no surprise that on the first day of fall practice, September 1, 1967, when student manager Morris Levy, known as Blondie, posted the tentative lineups on the Quonset hut, Isenbarger was listed as the number one quarterback along with another four possibilities on the depth chart, including Mike Perry, a capable running quarterback known as Redbird for his abundant shock of flaming red hair.

A young boy stared at the listing and finally found his name posted as the number three running back. He stood in front of the board and began to cry. Coach Brown threw his arms around the shoulders of the sophomore and said, "What's wrong little buddy?" The student replied, "Coach, I was recruited to play quarterback. I came here to play quarterback. I'm a quarterback." That young man was Harry Gonso.

CHAPTER 3

HARRY GONSO

Harry Gonso hailed from Findlay, Ohio. Not many did. Findlay, a town of thirty thousand, proudly known as "Flag City USA," was a way station for slaves making their way to Canada along the Underground Railroad in the days prior to the Civil War. In Gonso's day, travelers generally went the other way, south down the I-75 corridor en route from Toledo to Cincinnati for shopping and fine dining—and matchless high school football. Archbishop Moeller High School, a private, all-male, college preparatory school in the Cincinnati suburbs, sent dozens of its stars to Ohio State and other Division I programs. No one from Findlay was on the Ohio State roster in 1966.

There were six children spinning the lazy Susan at the Gonso family kitchen table. Harry was second in line to his sister Carol. Harry's father was a guidance counselor for Findlay High School. His mother was careful with the family budget. No matter; you didn't need a lot of money to enjoy fishing along the Blanchard River, pickup games, bicycle rides, and sleepovers in kid-friendly Findlay.

Gonso was a busy guy for the Findlay High School Trojans. He participated in football, swimming, and track and starred in baseball, to the extent that he was drafted by the Detroit Tigers and offered a $15,000 AA contract effective upon his high school graduation. He was a catcher with a slingshot arm. Hitting? Well, the scout said he would improve. None of his siblings were blessed with Gonso's athletic skills, nor did they care.

Gonso, "I'm a quarterback."

The Buckeye Conference was not even the second best football conference in the state. It featured towns most people never heard of, such as Elyria, Fostoria, Marion, and Mansfield. They played solid football in the Buckeye Conference, and Gonso, all 5'10" of him, exemplified the skill and the grit of this northern Ohio league. He could throw on the run and would rack up crazy yardage, sometimes as much as four hundred yards in a single game. Recruiters began to call, but many attributed Gonso's stats to a combination of a modicum of speed, sound coaching, and inferior competition.

Less than a tank of gas from Findlay was Columbus, the capital of Ohio, also the capital for Ohio football and often for the Midwest and the nation. Gonso dreamed of taking that jaunt and suiting up for coach Woody Hayes. Midway through his senior year, he was tantalized with a private lunch with Hayes, but the meeting failed to produce a scholarship offer. Hal Paul, Gonso's high school coach, contacted Purdue but the overture was not returned, and Notre Dame was not the least bit interested in an undersized quarterback of an okay team in a third-level league. Gonso didn't even look like a football player. His curly hair and horn-rimmed glasses invoked more of an image of a bookkeeper. Those recruiters misjudged the essence of Harry Gonso, an imaginative leader and a relentless and intense competitor.

Gonso graduated Findlay High with a grade-point average of three and change. He declined the Tigers' offer, knowing if he played baseball he would never attend college, never play football in the Big Ten, and never accomplish his ultimate goal of practicing law.

Only two Big Ten programs were willing to wager on the potential of Harry Gonso: Michigan State and Indiana. Neither made a strong bet, although Duffy Daugherty recruited Gonso beginning in his junior year and offered a scholarship. Michigan State was a perfect 7-0 in the Big Ten in 1965 and was ranked near the top of national polls throughout the year. Gonso agonized over his ability to play at that level. Perhaps the boy from Findlay was reaching too high. Coach Paul encouraged Gonso to attend Michigan State. It was rumored around the halls of Findlay High that Gonso was Paul's ticket to Daugherty's coaching staff. Gonso did not favor that cozy arrangement.

Gonso hedged his bet. At the urging of Nick Mourouzis, the

IU coach assigned to Gonso's recruitment, he spent a weekend at Indiana with Coach Pont. Like most Ohioans, Gonso revered Pont as a player and a coach. At the closing interview Pont said, "Harry, we really like you. We think you are a smart guy. You are a good athlete and you are a good leader but you are from Ohio and we are an Indiana school. We have offers to make to Indiana boys and the first Indiana boy that turns us down, you've got a scholarship."

Gonso stood up, extended his hand, and said, "Coach, I really like you an awful lot too but Michigan State likes me and they've offered me a scholarship and I'm going back home and accept it."

The next day he called Daugherty and said, "Thank you very much, I accept your offer." And then he had second thoughts.

Pont got it right. Gonso was a dynamic quarterback, but he was not a blue chipper. Given Indiana's miserable finishes in the Big Ten and its recent probation, Pont couldn't land many of his first choices. Gonso couldn't either. A week after the interview, Pont extended Gonso a scholarship. Gonso accepted and notified Michigan State that he had changed his mind. It was difficult for him to renege on his commitment and it plagued him for some time. Daugherty offered no argument.

Shortly after sorting out his college decision, Gonso noticed fellow Ohioan Karl Pankratz on television accepting an award as the state heavyweight high school wrestling champion. During the interview Pankratz declared that he was going to play linebacker for John Pont at Indiana University. Soon after the TV interview Gonso called Pankratz and said, "I'm going to Indiana. You want to drive there together?" On the way to Bloomington, the teammates-to-be discussed their similar Ohio backgrounds and their shared interest in football. They decided to room together.

Karl Pankratz was a star athlete at Saint Francis de Sales, an all-boys Catholic school in Toledo, Ohio. He lettered in baseball and football, but his real love was wrestling. His senior year he was undefeated. He credited wrestling with enhancing his balance, strength, and stamina, three important characteristics needed of a Division I football player. Like most football players with his talent, he played both ways, fullback and linebacker.

The wrestling finals were held on the Ohio State campus in St. John Arena. After his match, Woody Hayes pulled Pankratz into the locker room and offered him a scholarship, no letters, no visit, no romance. Pankratz had already been offered scholarships from Notre Dame, almost every Big Ten team, and many of the Mid-American Conference schools. Hayes's haphazard, almost arrogant late recruitment proved to be his undoing. Pankratz narrowed his choices to four schools: Michigan State, Indiana, Notre Dame, and Miami of Ohio.

Michigan State was the first university to be dropped from Pankratz's preferred list. On his visit to East Lansing, he watched the Spartans hold Ohio State to minus-32 yards rushing. In awe of Bubba Smith, Charlie Thornhill, and George Webster, he said to himself, "When am I ever going to get to play here?" When he was hosted at Miami of Ohio, he noted the esteem in which IU coach John Pont was held. His name, pictures, jersey, and other paraphernalia were featured in an exhibit of a Miami of Ohio hero. Pankratz said, "That's a man I could play for." He opted for Indiana because he admired Coach Pont, loved the campus, appreciated IU's academic reputation, and, as important as anything else, felt he could play right away.

Gonso arrived on campus confident that he would take snaps for John Pont, right up until the day he found himself as the number three running back on the Quonset hut wall. It was clear then that the coaching staff favored Isenbarger, but Gonso had a few advantages. Gonso's high school backfield coach, Doug Rice, had played quarterback for University of Cincinnati, and he taught Gonso the subtle tricks of quarterbacking: how to square your shoulders and throw on the run, where to place your hands under the center to receive the ball, how to ride the center, how to keep your head up and never show where you are going, and many other nuances and techniques that Isenbarger had not learned. Gonso could not match Isenbarger's size, athletic ability, and skill diversity, but he had polish and more intense competitive instincts. A rivalry raged. When questioned, Pont smiled and complimented both players. The press, the fans, the players could only guess who would prevail, and they often did guess.

Gonso and Pankratz discussed the battle often well past midnight. One night just as they were falling asleep the boys were awakened in their dorm room by a few upperclassmen, who invited Pankratz to join their fraternity, Sigma Alpha Epsilon. Pankratz insisted, "I am not joining SAE unless Harry has a chance to join as well." A second invitation was promptly issued and promptly accepted. Other teammates including Terry Cole, Mike Perry, and Eric Stolberg also joined SAE. The last day before summer vacation, Pankratz injured his knee wrestling in the fraternity house, but he didn't tell the coaches or anyone else. He didn't realize it at the time, but he had torn cartilage. He thought all summer that the injury would go away, but it didn't.

On September 10, 1967, two weeks before the season opener with Kentucky, Blondie posted the lineups on the Quonset hut. Junior Al Gage was a tight end as expected. He was a streamlined 6'3" who could measure out at 6'4" when he stood up straight. He was sure-handed and fast, and anyone wishing to play tight end at IU would have to play behind Al Gage. Gage was Pont's first recruit. His play for East Saint Louis Senior High caught the attention of recruiters from Indiana, Nebraska, and Kansas State. Gage, the seventh of twelve children, could not afford college and was deciding on a military enlistment when his coach said he was good enough at football for a free ride, a full scholarship.

Coach Brown picked him up at the airport on a sunny spring day in 1965. As they drove over the rolling hills of southern Indiana, Gage thought, "Oh, my God, this is gorgeous. I have died and gone to heaven." Coach Pont was offered the coaching position that same weekend. They met at Memorial Stadium. Pont extended a hand and said, "Al, I'm coming to IU. Join me." The deal was closed on that handshake. After the 1966 season, Gage appeared on television with Pont and predicted that IU would go to the Rose Bowl the following year. Pont was incredulous.

Nate Cunningham was posted at defensive halfback. He was also one of Pont's early recruits. Cunningham grew up in Danville, Illinois, with three options, the factory, the military, or football. The choice was easy. Coach Brown had come to Danville High School to watch Cunningham play, and he insisted that Pont offer him a scholarship. When Cunningham spent a weekend in Bloomington, he knew he would not go anywhere else. He waited by the mailbox for the confirmation to arrive.

Dave Kornowa had earned his spot as a defensive halfback. Kornowa was recruited out of Toledo, where he played quarterback and defensive back and doubled as a punter and a placekicker. He was recruited to IU as a quarterback, but he switched to defensive back his sophomore year and then switched back to quarterback his junior year to back up Frank Stavroff. After another switch, he was back to the defensive backfield for his senior year. Kornowa won ten varsity letters and was all-city in three sports: basketball, baseball, and football. He wasn't even six feet tall but he was quick and tough, and he hit with the force of a rampaging buffalo.

When his father asked him what school he chose among the many that offered scholarships, he said, "Indiana." When asked why, he said, "I said Indiana because I want to play in the Rose Bowl." His father snickered. Kornowa had no idea that Indiana had never gone to the Rose Bowl, but Phil Dickens had sold him on that possibility. But for all his skill, Kornowa often went into the game without passion, even after a Pont pep talk, whose rhetoric could make you run out the door before opening it. He never got excited before the game or through the predrills. He often wondered whether he was ready to play, but as soon as he got hit the first time he turned into a villain.

One afternoon after practice, Kornowa walked down the field

toward the locker room with Coach Pont. Pont glanced over to his starting defensive halfback and said, "Well, who do you think I should put at quarterback?"

Kornowa didn't hesitate, "If you want to go to the Rose Bowl, it's Harry Gonso."

Brown Marks was posted as a starting linebacker. He was a 6'2", 210-pound senior from Eva Gordon High School in Magnolia, Mississippi, who arrived in Bloomington at age sixteen. He played football and baseball, and he played saxophone in the band. The previous year he was a regular at defensive end and was one of the team's leading tacklers with 27 solos and 34 assists. His teammates respected him as one of the most aggressive members of the defensive unit.

When Marks suffered a hamstring injury in practice, the role was assigned to Bob Moynihan, who was small for a linebacker—6' and 180 pounds. He was out of Hammond, Indiana, playing for mediocre teams at Hammond Clark High School. His high school coach Al Peterson had played with Coach Brown on the 1945 team. Moynihan was not recruited nor was he offered a scholarship. He was one of approximately seventy-five young men who went out for football as freshmen, about half of whom were walk-ons. Moynihan felt his future looked pretty dim. He said to himself, "I'm so far down on the depth chart that nothing is going to be happening here for me." But because of his love of football, he stuck it out trying to make the team as a receiver. When spring practice arrived, he was switched to the defense despite his size. He started more than half of the games in 1966, his sophomore year.

Isenbarger, a victim of his own diverse talent, was listed as tailback—a tailback for whom Pont would inscribe in the playbook combinations of sweeps and passes that utilized Isenbarger's running and passing skills.

As for quarterback, it was Gonso.

With the lineups set, Pont's football players were beginning to jell. Pont was pleased with his linemen. The intense training routine was paying off, particularly on defense, where Crusan's crew was agile and more energetic. Pont put them to a personal test. He put on a helmet and ran halfback in full contact drills. (He waited until the end of a day of hard-hitting practice.) More than a decade removed from his best playing days, he had maintained optimum weight and was still a premier-level halfback—elusive and fast. After Pont avoided yet another tackle, Kaczmarek said in the huddle, "That halfback is mighty quick. Don't let him do that to us." The defense responded, but Pont just came harder. Crusan pronounced, "That old man can still play!" Pont strutted back to the huddle. Finally, Kaczmarek and Duffy read a play just right, and they both hit Pont, hard. His watch, a prize from participation in the Tangerine Bowl, shattered, and the pieces flew through the air as if propelled in slow motion. Pont, dabbing at a bloody lip, glared at his linebackers with his dark, intense eyes. The exercise was discontinued for the day. Blondie found as many pieces as he could and took them to a local jeweler. The watch was never the same.

The offensive line, anchored by fifth-year seniors Bob Russell and Harold Mauro, had much to be proud of despite the team's record in the past two years. Not only did they, along with fellow lineman Doug Crusan, give Frank Stavroff time to break IU and Big Ten records with his arm, but they also opened holes for Mike Krivoshia, who in 1966 was the second leading rusher in the Big Ten. Krivoshia grew up along the Ohio River in Beaver County, Pennsylvania. He earned MVP honors as a Midland High School Leopard in football and track, where he threw the shot put and ran sprints. At 6' and 214 pounds, he was a bruising up-the-middle fullback. If a hole was there, he would find it and blast his way through. Bob Russell, Harold Mauro, and Doug Crusan, along with Rick Spickard and Gary Cassells, made sure it was there. IU landed Krivoshia despite major recruiting efforts by Ohio State, Michigan, and Penn State.

Harold Mauro grew up in Verona, a small steel town in Pennsylvania, and attended the smallest school in western

Pennsylvania. There were forty-two in his graduating class, yet they won a Class D state championship his senior year, and he was recruited by a number of schools. On a recruiting trip to Alabama, he was hosted by Joe Namath and Leroy Jordan. When it was time to leave, coach Bear Bryant said, "You want to play for me don't you." Mauro, an impressionable seventeen-year-old, said, "Sure" and signed a commitment letter. When he returned home, his father counseled young Harold to look around a little bit. Mauro visited Purdue, Michigan State, Michigan, and then Indiana. He thought Indiana was a good fit. Bear Bryant lost a warrior, but few knew. Mauro was nicknamed "Monk" by his neighbor because his quiet and reserved demeanor reminded the neighbor of life in a monastery. On the football field, though, Monk was transformed into a hostile force. Monk enjoyed his friends and was game for pranks and antics. One evening he and two buddies drove to the Jackson County Fair in Brownstown, a town of fewer than two thousand people about thirty miles south of Bloomington. At the fair one could win money by wrestling a bear or removing a monkey hanging from a bar. Monk chose the monkey, which weighed about a hundred pounds. The carnival barker offered ten dollars to anyone who could dislodge the monkey. The monkey was so distressed it did what monkeys often do. After three attempted tackles, Monk finally was successful and was paid in full, but his clothes smelled so bad that his companions forced him to leave them on the roadside and ride back to Bloomington in his underwear.

Pont had the horses but he didn't have a team—not yet. He remembered the 1949 squad at Miami University, a team that played for each other. They were not just teammates but friends and allies. One morning after breakfast, he shared his concern with junior trainer Dean Kleinschmidt. Kleinschmidt was one of those rare young men who knew exactly what he wanted to be from the first day he entered college, maybe even sooner. He sought to make his career as an athletic trainer and was enrolled in a course of study that would lead to a bachelor's degree in health and safety with a major in athletic training. IU was the only college in the country to offer this major. Kleinschmidt suffered from asthma, and although he was a good athlete, he did not possess the skills or size necessary to play football at the Division I level; nonetheless, he exhibited an enthusiasm and team spirit that was infectious in the locker room.

Kleinschmidt had spent the summer of 1967 with the Green Bay Packers. Earlier in the year, the Packers had won the first AFL-NFL World Championship game, known retroactively as Super Bowl I, humiliating Kansas City 35-10. As an athletic trainer, young Kleinschmidt literally rubbed shoulders with legendary quarterback Bart Starr and linebacker Ray Nitschke. Pont asked Kleinschmidt to share some of his experiences at Green Bay. At a team meeting, Kleinschmidt said about the Packers, "They love one another."

Gonso looked at Pankratz with an inquiring expression: "What is he trying to say?"

The coaches exchanged quizzical glances. Kleinschmidt stood up on a chair and continued, "The Packers stand up, hold hands, and sing an old gospel song together. Why don't we do that?"

With a little cajoling everyone stood up and grabbed the hand next to him. Kleinschmidt started to sing,

> He's got the whole world in His hands,
> He's got the whole world in His hands,
> He's got the whole world in His hands,
> He's got the whole world in His hands,
>
> He's got my brothers and my sisters in His hands,
> He's got my brothers and my sisters in His hands,
> He's got my brothers and my sisters in His hands,
> He's got the whole world in His hands.

He riffed,
> He's got the best linebackers in His hands,
> He's got the best linemen in His hands,
> He's got the best receivers in His hands,
> He's got the whole world in His hands.

With a little prodding, senior Cordell Gill added some verses. Finally, Kleinschmidt verbalized the ultimate quest of the IU team:
> He's got the Rose Bowl Champions in His hands,
> He's got the Rose Bowl Champions in His hands,
> He's got the Rose Bowl Champions in His hands,
> He's got the whole world in His hands.

Sometimes a corny situation becomes a key moment in the history of a football season. It was that evening when younger guys and veterans started to become a team. And as a team they needed to be ready. Waiting for them on September 23 was their first opponent of the season, the University of Kentucky. A record-breaking opening day crowd would be on their feet in anticipation of the 1967 season and of better days to come.

1967 Indiana Schedule

Date	Opponent
September 23*	Kentucky
September 30*	Kansas
October 7	Illinois
October 14*	Iowa
October 21	Michigan
October 23	Arizona
November 4*	Wisconsin
November 11	Michigan State
November 18	Minnesota
November 25*	Purdue

*Home Games

Harry Gonso

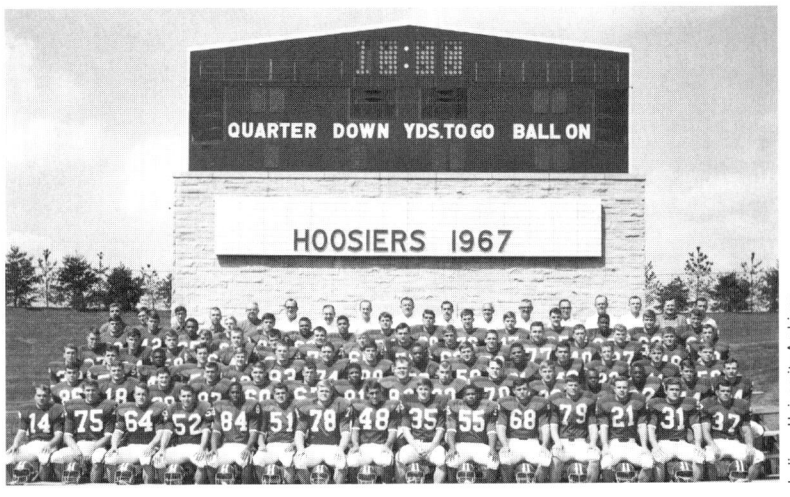

(Front row, L to R) *Dave Kornowa, Doug Rhodus, Bob Russell, Kenneth Kaczmarek, Brown Marks, Harold Mauro, Doug Crusan, Terry Cole, Mike Krivoshia, Cordell Gill, Gary Cassells, Rick Spickard, Gary Nichols, Bill Huff, and Kevin Duffy.*
(2nd row, L to R) *Bill McCaa, Mike Perry, Bob Moynihan, Al Kamradt, Jerry Grecco, Pat Egan, Al Gage, John Carlson, Tom Bilunas, Bill Bergman, Dave Evans, Cal Wilson, Nate Cunningham, Roger Grover, and Bob Douglass.*
(3rd row, L to R) *Mike Baughman, Steve Applegate, Mike Adams, Gayle Robinson, George Wortley, Jim Sniadecki, Al Schmidt, Bob Long, Bob Kirk, Mike Roth, Cal Snowden, Dick Waltz, Ken Long, Bill Chiz, and Bill Bordner.*
(4th row, L to R) *Bill Wolfe, Dave Hoehn, Steve Gruber, Harry Gonso, Mike Deal, Bob Nichols, Don Ghrist, Bob Geers, Harold Dunn, Don DeSalle, Tom DeMarco, John David, Jade Butcher, Dick Bozicevich, Frank Canarecci, and Jay Mathias.*
(5th row, L to R) *Tom Warriner, Don Warner, Greg Thaxton, Eric Stolberg, Bill Simon, Clarence Price, Ben Norman, Karl Pankratz, Bill Paulus, Ed Harrison, John Isenbarger, Walter Jurkiewicz, Charlie Murphy, E.G. White, and Fred Mitchell.*
(Last row, L to R) *Manager John Rabold, manager Mike Dumke, manager Blondie Levy, assistant trainer Steve Moore, equipment manager Red Grow, coach Charley McDaniel, coach Howard Brown, coach Jake Van Schoyck, coach Herb Fairfield, coach Jay Fry, head coach John Pont, coach Ernie Plank, coach Nick Mourouzis, coach Bob Hicks, coach Bob Baker, head trainer Warren Ariail, and assistant Ted Verlihay*

CHAPTER 4

KENTUCKY

On Friday, September 23, 1967, the day before Indiana's encounter with Kentucky, Pont bused his team to McCormick's Creek State Park, a pristine wilderness homesteaded 150 years before by John McCormick and a perfect place to shield his team from distraction and attractions. McCormick's Creek was dedicated as Indiana's first state park on July 4, 1916, as part of the state's centennial celebration. Originally one hundred acres, the park continued to grow through the acquisition of surrounding farms and homesteads as they came up for sale. Pont gathered his team in this quiet environment to prepare them for the battle ahead. McCormick's Creek was a perfect choice, with hiking trails, waterfalls, caves, and wild game. At the park, the Canyon Inn provided rustic but first-rate accommodations and full service dining to the taste of this group of more than sixty hungry men. Steaks were the order of the day. Pont delivered his squad to the stadium the next day two hours before game time, as would be his custom for every home contest.

The Hoosier faithful turned out to see Indiana and Kentucky resume their rivalry after a forty-year lapse. It seemed all of

Bloomington and half of Lexington filled the fifty thousand seats in Memorial Stadium, part of the largest opening game attendance in IU history. Up in his suite overlooking the fifty-yard line, President Stahr entertained prominent alumni. Stahr was born in Hickman, Kentucky, and was the former dean of the UK Law School. Although he professed to be rooting for the Cream and Crimson, some wondered. They need not have.

It was a dazzling sunny autumn day as the campus began to show off its colors. Kentucky didn't pay much attention to that. The Wildcats were intent on improving their 3-6-1 record of 1966, and coach Charlie Bradshaw, who had never lost an opening game during his six years at Kentucky, had them ready. Indiana, a program that managed only three wins in the previous two years, was a three-point betting favorite. The oddsmakers failed to consider that Kentucky was on the trimester system and began practice on August 19, giving them thirteen more practice days than IU, which was confined to its September 1 opening day.

On the fifth play of the game, Kentucky quarterback and team captain Dicky Lyons sent halfback Roger Gann through the Indiana line. Nate Cunningham reached for Gann and came up with a piece of his jersey. Gann sprinted for 56 yards and a touchdown, not a great debut for Doug Crusan and the defensive line. Three minutes after the last strains of "On the Banks of the Wabash" echoed through the stadium, Kentucky led 7-0. Lyons turned to Coach Bradshaw and said, "We're going to kill 'em."

Orwig paced the press box commiserating with whoever would listen. Pont raged at Cunningham, waved his arms, and tossed his red thermos full of coffee. The team realized this was not practice but a real battle with a determined opponent. There were to be no more easy Kentucky touchdowns that afternoon. On Indiana's first possession, they drove to the Kentucky 31-yard line, where Don Warner's field goal attempt was blocked. The Kentucky defense, desperate to preserve its seven-point lead, smothered Gonso and his backfield for the rest of the first half, preventing Indiana from mounting another reliable drive.

With less than two minutes left in the first half, Terry Cole gifted Kentucky with a fumble on the Indiana 28-yard line that led to a 33-yard field goal five plays later. Pont paced the sideline in a fury. The teams went into the locker rooms with the score 10-0, Kentucky.

When Pont got fired up, few coaches could be rougher. Pont had been compared to Paul Bryant of Alabama and Frank Leahy of Notre Dame. It was said of Leahy that two days after a game, he reviewed film with his team. When they came to a missed block, Leahy had the operator run the play over again, then again. He flicked on the lights, stared at the guilty player, and said, "I'm going to run this film one more time. If you miss the block this time you can turn in your uniform."

Pont was fired up. In a ten-minute halftime tirade he cited missed assignments, haphazard tackles, and otherwise lethargic play. Very few players escaped his torment, particularly Nate Cunningham. Pont, who appreciated Cunningham's sense of football and thought that he would one day coach, said more than a few times, "Nate, you can do better." Cunningham, an African American, referred to Pont as an equal opportunity ass kicker. Shortly before the second half began, Pont arose and bellowed, "When are you guys going to believe? You are a great football team. When are you guys going to believe?" At his feet was the Bell and Howell projector used to review game films. Pont dropkicked that projector across the room. Sprockets, reels, wheels, bulbs, and lenses exploded upon impact. Parts flew everywhere.

Pont repeated, "When are you guys going to believe?"

In the silence that followed Crusan whispered, "We all believe."

The team rose as a group and charged the door. In his postgame comments, Coach Bradshaw of Kentucky said, "I thought Indiana was much more enthused and determined when the teams came out to start the second half."

Cinderella Ball

It was a different scene in the Kentucky locker room. Bradshaw hugged his team and congratulated them for their effort. He ended his pep talk with, "Our half is coming up."

Outside the fieldhouse, some downtrodden fans trudged back to their vehicles to wash down the remainder of their ribs and chicken with a few cold beers and beat the traffic home. Those who did not return missed the actual debut performance of the 1967 IU football team.

Snowden (61) and Crusan (78) in a defensive effort.

Gonso (16) ready to launch.

In the third quarter, Kentucky began a march toward another touchdown. Rather than pad the lead with a field goal on fourth down from IU's 29-yard line, Bradshaw sent in a hook pattern pass play. Karl Pankratz read it easily and stepped in front for the interception. A few plays later, Gonso floated a screen pass to John Isenbarger who dashed 42 yards to the Kentucky 18. On fourth down, Gonso hit Jade Butcher, who was standing all alone in the right side of the end zone waiting for the ball—a first college touchdown for Gonso and for Butcher. In the excitement of the moment, the Don Warner extra point attempt was missed, and the score was 10-6 Kentucky.

A more comfortable Gonso began to display some of that flash he was famous for back in Findlay. On the second play of IU's next possession, Gonso swept 63 yards up the left sideline. Credit that run to John Isenbarger, who interrupted the glide path of a Kentucky defender with a vicious block. *Indiana Daily Student* sports editor Rick Roth wrote that Isenbarger "is a young man who goes through life as if he were two steps ahead of a forest fire." After the game Isenbarger said, "I never played a football game at any other spot than quarterback. I had to learn how to block. I realized you have to hit them low and they'll go down no matter how big they are." He added, "I don't care where I play just as long as I can play."

Gonso failed to advance the ball on the next three plays. On fourth down at the Kentucky eight-yard line, Gonso, running for his life, threw a perfect touchdown pass to Al Gage. No sooner than one referee shot up his arms to signify a touchdown than his colleague threw his flag to nullify the play and patted his head to signify the infraction was an ineligible receiver downfield. The fifteen-yard penalty erased the touchdown and brought the ball back to the 23-yard line. A field goal would close the gap to 10-9. Gage implored Gonso to run the same play: "Hey, let's do it again. We'll catch it Harry." Gonso unloaded another touchdown pass, this time to split end Eric Stolberg, normally a secondary target, who stood waiting in the end zone. As the ball descended, Kentucky safety

Bobby Abbott, a 5'8", undersized leaper, knocked him flat and at the same time tipped the ball back up into the air. Stolberg, on his back, looked up and thought, "Oh, geez." Gage was the secondary receiver on the play. Receivers coach Bob Baker stressed in practice, "If you're the secondary receiver, go out in the area and don't just sit still. Bug around." Gage was "bugging around" when he saw the ball thrown toward Stolberg. He headed in that direction to throw a block if it was needed. He had his eye on the ball all the way and when it was tipped he knew right away he could get to it. It fell into his hands and he hugged it as he fell to the ground. Touchdown! Isenbarger, on the two-point conversion that would have protected the IU lead from a Kentucky field goal, failed when his knee touched down two yards in front of the goal line. The score was 12-10 Indiana.

In the fourth quarter, Kentucky went to the air and was punished with three interceptions. Nate Cunningham redeemed himself with one of those grabs when he wrested the ball from a Kentucky receiver. Kornowa intercepted Kentucky twice, both times on short passes to Kornowa's left. The quarterback made a bad pass on both of them. Each time, Kornowa went up and one-handed the ball, stopped it, and pulled it down. A fourth-quarter Indiana drive was blunted when Gonso lost a fumble on the Kentucky 38-yard line. The game ended without further scoring.

In the locker room, Gonso deadpanned he wasn't really worried at halftime. "I called most of the plays and just felt that I could bring the team back. I am sure Coach Pont has a lot more to do on the sidelines than be bothered with calling plays."

Bob Collins responded in his *Star* column, "If Pont affirms that Gonso called most of the plays put me down as a believer. No coach in his right mind would have made some of those calls." He said of Gonso, "He can't run so awful fast and anytime he throws the ball more than 15 yards he is pleading for help from the Holy Ghost but that doesn't seem to bother Harry, so why should it bother us?"

Pont countered, "I don't think there's a better sophomore quarterback in the country than Gonso." He added, "And Gage is the best tight end in the Big Ten." A more sober Charlie Bradshaw said after the game that he felt Kentucky would wear Indiana down in the latter stages of the game, but it was the other way around. Perhaps Bradshaw watched too many IU films from 1965 and 1966.

The super sophomores—Butcher, Isenbarger, and Gonso—met Pont's expectation, but it was a victory to be credited to the entire team. Mike Krivoshia made significant contributions with strong efforts in short-yardage situations. Collins cracked that the defensive backfield, which in recent years had ranked second only to the Italian army in the achievement division, contributed more than its fair share to the triumph. Collins summed it up for the *Indianapolis Star*: "Indiana showed a commendable belief in their ability to get the job done. In football, determination and desire can go a long way toward molding a solid football unit." Had he known, Collins may have added that singing together also helps mold a solid football unit.

Al Gage had to catch two touchdowns to score one. Gage was a student of the game who listened to and trusted Coach Baker. And why not? Baker was quarterback of the undefeated Ball State University team in 1949. As coach of Madison Heights High School in Anderson, he produced an undefeated team in 1965 and a string of fourteen straight victories.

Gonso completed 11 of 15 passes for 121 yards and both of IU's touchdowns. He picked up another 115 yards on 25 carries off the option play. For his work that Saturday afternoon, he was selected as the United Press International Back of the Week in his first varsity game. Gonso's biggest moment was after the game when he saw how delighted his coach was with the victory. Gonso said, "I've never seen a man so happy. Right then I would have given my scholarship away to see him that elated after ten games."

Few people outside of Kentucky and Indiana took more

than a passing notice of Gonso's performance and this contest between two teams from which not much was expected. Another game loomed a week away: the University of Kansas was coming to town.

CHAPTER 5

KANSAS

Kansas labored in the Big Eight Conference—labored because throughout the 1950s and early 1960s, the conference could have been called the Big One and Little Seven. Bud Wilkinson's juggernaut at Oklahoma dominated the competition. It was rare that any Big Eight team or any other team defeated Oklahoma on the gridiron. Wilkinson's record in Norman was 145-29-4, including winning 47 straight games. In the 1960s, Kansas developed a lore of its own, posting a record of 7-2-1 in 1960 and a Bluebonnet Bowl victory in 1961. All-American John Hadl led the team both of those years. In 1963 and 1964, Kansas boasted one of the most exciting college broken field runners since the invention of the game, Gale Sayers. Sayers's career was chronicled in *Brian's Song*, a movie about Sayers's relationship with his roommate, halfback Brian Piccolo, during Piccolo's professional football career with the Chicago Bears. It is said that *Brian's Song* is one of the few movies that can make a grown man cry.

Like Indiana, Kansas had not fared well in the previous few years. In 1966, the Jayhawks had gone winless in conference play and had managed only two victories for the second year in a row. Oddsmakers took note of the sizzle in Indiana's second-half comeback and improbable final touchdown against Kentucky and installed IU as a six-point favorite in this first-ever meeting between these two teams. Kansas came into the game 0-1, but those numbers could easily have been reversed had Kansas not tried mightily to give their game away to a mediocre Stanford team and finally succeeded 21-20. Halfback Junior Riggins, a former prep dash champion, fumbled on the opening kickoff, giving Stanford the ball on the Kansas 24-yard line. The Jayhawks lost the ball twice more on fumbles and three times on interceptions. Kansas was penalized seven times during the game, including on an illegal procedure call that nullified a touchdown at the end of the first half. Finally, with only two minutes left in the game, they missed a chip shot field goal that would have given them the victory. Coach "Pepper" Rodgers, former assistant at UCLA in his first season at Lawrence, inherited flanker Donnie Shanklin, halfback Junior Riggins, and quarterback Bobby Douglass, all capable of explosive breakthroughs. In the Stanford game, Shanklin returned a punt 47 yards and caught two passes for 65 yards, and Riggins returned a punt 87 yards. The Kansas defense was anchored by a behemoth, 6'8", 250-pound Vernon Vanoy at defensive end, whose wingspan made it easy for him to terrorize opposing quarterbacks. After plaguing helpless runners during football season, Vanoy was a formidable center on the Kansas basketball team.

Friday, September 29, was a beautiful relaxing day at McCormick's Creek. The team members enjoyed strolls along the ten miles of park or relaxed by the fireplace at the Canyon Inn. After a steak dinner, team members broke into groups according to position. Linebacker Kevin Duffy and the rest of the defensive backfield met with Coach Plank to discuss strategy, Kansas stars to watch, and keys to stopping quarterback Bobby Douglass. Although it was early in the evening, Duffy went upstairs for a good night's sleep before game day. He pulled down his covers and found a turd under his pillow. He ran back downstairs and asked Isenbarger, Harry's roommate, "Do you know anything about Harry putting a turd under my pillow?"

Isenbarger replied, "Yep, he did it."

Kevin demanded, "Okay, give me the key to your room."

The next morning at the end of breakfast Duffy snuck into Gonso's room, zipped open his dopp kit, and took a big dump without toilet paper. He closed it and squished it all together and put the dopp kit back in its neat little place. Then Duffy thought, "This kid's going to be all upset about this and we're going to lose the game and it's going to be my fault." Gonso showed no ill effects. He suspected Isenbarger ratted on him, but he never found out for sure.

Isenbarger (17) chased by 6'8", 250-pound Vernon Vanoy (84).

Cinderella Ball

September 30 was another warm autumn afternoon and another frightening start for the Hoosiers. In the first quarter, Gonso lost the ball on his own two-yard line when accosted by the monstrous Vanoy. (Gonso took great pains to avoid him the rest of the game.) After the game, Gonso described his confrontation with Vanoy as a frightful experience. In the first play after the Gonso strip, quarterback Bobby Douglass kept the ball for a touchdown, and before the Hoosier faithful could recover, cagey Bobby Douglass ran a fake kick and sent Shanklin across the goal line for a two-point conversion.

With less than four minutes remaining in the first half, Gonso finally lit a match to his offense with a couple of passes to Gage. He caught one but was prevented from a sure catch of the other one by a Kansas defender, who paid with a penalty that brought the ball to the Kansas 28-yard line. On the halfback option, Isenbarger took a pitch from Gonso and threw to Butcher three feet from the goal line. Butcher turned and high-stepped across. Gonso hit Isenbarger with the two-point conversion. In two consecutive scoring plays, Isenbarger threw one and caught one for a total of eight points, tying the score at halftime, 8-8.

Ray Marquette, sportswriter for the *Indianapolis Star*, said the Hoosiers came out of the tunnel breathing fire at the start of the third quarter. The interns had made sure that Pont had no more machinery and equipment to destroy, but Pont needed no props to deliver a strong diatribe beseeching his players to beat up on this cream puff. In the opening minutes of the second half, the Hoosiers were moving the ball when Vanoy, smelling red meat, again caught up with the terrified Gonso. But this time those long arms got tangled up in Gonso's facemask. The ensuing penalty, along with a driving run by Terry Cole and another brilliant reception by Butcher, brought the team to the nine-yard line. On the next play, Gonso lobbed the ball to Butcher for Butcher's second touchdown of the day. Dave Kornowa subbed for Don Warner and his arthritic toe and kicked the extra point. Warner played at a variety of positions for Andrean High School in Gary, Indiana. At IU, in addition to kicking extra points, Warner played on the kickoff team.

Douglass showed why he was an All-American. He went right after Indiana and scored a touchdown to tie the score at 15. Two series later, Indiana was stalled on the Kansas 10-yard line. Kornowa squirmed on the bench trying to stay loose and relaxed for a field goal attempt. He couldn't do it. When his name was called, he lined up, worried and anxious that he might miss the most important kick of his college career. He had nothing to worry about. The field goal gave the Hoosiers an 18-15 lead.

Douglass threatened again but safety Mike Baughman stalled a Kansas drive with an interception of a tipped ball on the Indiana 12-yard line. Later Kansas had one more chance on a 37-yard field goal attempt. The ball sailed away to the left of the uprights and took along with it Kansas' opportunity for victory. The final score was 18-15. On the way to his car for a long ride back to Lawrence, a frustrated Jayhawk fan quipped to his friends all dressed in Kansas blue and crimson, "Call Pepper. Ask him to put Ryun on the team. No one's gonna catch him." He was referring to Kansas schoolboy Jim Ryun, who had set the world record in the mile earlier in the year.

Running back Terry Cole averaged just short of four and a half yards per carry on 14 attempts due in large part to the play of seasoned linemen center Harold Mauro and guards Bob Russell and Gary Cassells. Cole said he was confident going up the middle: "The line was opening up big holes for me and I knew they would be there." According to *Indianapolis Star* assistant sports editor John Bansch, Bob Russell and Gary Cassells "are one of the best offensive guard combinations in Big Ten football this fall." According to Bansch, Russell, whom the players called "Bull," was always thinking ahead and studied the men he would have to block, whereas Cassells was quicker and stronger and made on-the-spot adjustments to achieve his blocks. Russell at 6' and 218 pounds was an outstanding lineman at Mansfield High School in Ohio who spurned an offer from Cincinnati before enrolling at Indiana as a premed student. Russell qualified for fifth-year red shirt status by having to sit out in 1964 after knee surgery. His academic burden included ten hours of graduate courses. He planned to forgo a professional football career and enter medical school the following year. Cassells, a 6'3", 212-pound senior from Conard High School in West Hartford, Connecticut, could have opted out of football in 1967 due to an injured shoulder that would require postseason surgery. He opted to play but was excused from contact drills Monday through Wednesday for fear of aggravating his injury. Coaches limited him to running and working on individual technique. On Thursday he was allowed to hit just enough to get used to the contact for Saturday. Cassells wanted to practice with the team and longed for the contact, the hitting that is so much a part of football. In his place during practice and as backup during games was E. G. White, a 6'1", 215-pound sophomore from South Bend Riley High School. White also played on kickoffs and punt returns.

Gonso (16) runs for his life.

Baughman's fourth-quarter interception saved the day for IU. Baughman didn't look like a football player. At 6'3" he weighed barely 170 pounds. He was skinny, breakable. Skinny players usually do not belong on the gridiron. Baughman not only belonged—he excelled. At Lancaster High School in Ohio, he played football, baseball, and basketball and was offered Division I college scholarships in all three sports. In football he played split end and safety and was named Ohio Lineman of the Year. He was one of ten prep stars honored in an appearance on the Ed Sullivan Show. Woody Hayes drove the forty-five minutes from Columbus to meet Mike and his parents in their living room, just as he had done with Mike's two older brothers, also star athletes. Hayes failed to land any of them. For Mike, Ohio State University was too big. The student body was larger than his hometown. Indiana was just right.

In the freshman game the previous year against Ohio State, Baughman had three interceptions. After one he was chased down before he could run the ball back for a touchdown. As he got up, there was Woody, who said, "Glad you didn't come to OSU; you're too slow."

Baughman was one of a few athletes who played two sports at Indiana University. He played center field for the varsity baseball team all three years of his eligibility. Never had so much athleticism been housed in a skinnier frame.

The hometown press was upbeat and congratulatory, but a skeptical Ray Marquette noted that IU had won its first two games by a total margin of five points. He wrote in the *Indianapolis Star*, "No one, especially Pont, is about to predict a run for the Big Ten championship this fall."

Bill and Jane Orwig invited a few friends over for supper after the game. Pont and some of the coaches and their wives joined the Orwigs to celebrate the first 2-0 start in recent memory. The Ponts walked over from their house just a few doors down Heritage Woods Road. When the party settled down, Orwig and Pont found a chance to talk. Pont drained his second scotch and said, "Bill, I may have made a lousy mistake when I repositioned Doug Crusan from one of the best offensive linemen in the country and set him up for failure on our defensive line. He had a horrible game against Kentucky, and he was not much better today. In spite of intense coaching at practice, Crusan is still playing like an offensive lineman." Orwig and Pont knew that an offensive lineman's duty is to engage the defense for as long as he can in order to protect the quarterback. You hit, you stay, you drive, you turn your body and your opponents. But a defensive lineman's assignment is just the opposite. You say, "I don't want to have anything to do with you. I've got to get going. You disengage, and with the help of the linebackers, find and stop the man with the ball."

Before Orwig had a chance to reply, Pont added, "I have decided to give the arrangement another game."

Pont was desperate for Crusan to figure this out before the Big Ten opener next Saturday in Champaign-Urbana against the fighting Illini. Pont was 2-0, his best start at IU. Victory was sweet. He wanted more, and Crusan and the defensive line were key.

CHAPTER 6
ILLINOIS

The Hoosiers bused into Memorial Stadium in Champaign-Urbana on October 6, 1967, in the afternoon before their Big Ten opener with Illinois the next day. For decades IU had been a patsy for Illinois, who led the series 30-7-2. The previous year the losing score was 24-10.

The nucleus of the team that busted IU in 1966 returned. That included flamboyant wide receiver John Wright, who had posted eight receptions in the first two outings of Illinois in the 1967 season. In the 1966 game with IU, Wright caught nine passes for 116 yards and two touchdowns, an Illinois career receiving record. One of those touchdowns was for 65 yards, with Wright running the last 25 yards holding the ball way in the air. All week long the defensive team had to watch that tape again and again. By kickoff, Kaczmarek and his crew of marauding linebackers hated that Illini, and all the rest of them. Illinois also boasted promising quarterback Bob Naponic, fullback Rich Johnson, and fierce defensive lineman Fritz Harms. The Indiana coaches felt that Illinois was a stronger team than Kentucky or Kansas. The oddsmakers agreed. Indiana was a three-point underdog.

Circumstances were vastly different for the Illinois program in 1967, however. In 1966, athletic director Doug Mills announced his retirement. The assistant athletic director, Mel Brewer, seemed the likely successor until football coach Pete Elliott applied for the position. Elliott was the popular choice because he had won the Rose Bowl for Illinois in 1963. Fans never forget that, and administrators rarely do. Brewer, in a snit, blew the whistle on Mills and Elliott—and himself. He told university president David Henry of a surreptitious slush fund he administered for the basketball and football programs. Henry wasted no time in contacting the Big Ten commissioner about those nefarious activities. Approximately thirty athletes were investigated, and in the end seven athletes were suspended. Under threat of suspension from the Big Ten, the University of Illinois fired basketball coach Harry Combes, assistant basketball coach Howard Braun, and head football coach Pete Elliott.
    First-year coach Jim Valek's squad came into the game after manhandling Pittsburgh the week before, 34-6. The home crowd of well over fifty thousand held hope that Valek was the answer to the redemption of the University of Illinois.
    The IU team suffered a setback on the day before leaving for Champaign-Urbana for the Illinois game. In a live drill practice, starting linebacker Bob Moynihan was double teamed and pushed backwards. When his leg got caught under him, it snapped his fibula just above the ankle. He was lost for the season. Brown Mark's hamstring was on the mend, and he reassumed his starter designation.
    Pont was gratified to know his recruiting and coaching strategies had paid off with two opening season victories, but he approached the Illinois game with the realization that little counted until the Big Ten season. Every Big Ten football coach knew that. Little else mattered. Pont was serious in his recruiting comments to Stolberg and others. His success would be measured on his ability to win the Big Ten and go to the Rose Bowl, and he intended to do exactly that. Illinois was the first stop. The team sensed the tension. After a light workout

Illinois

and walk-through late Friday afternoon, the team assembled in the visitor's locker room. Outside it was raining and dreary. In the dead quiet Cal Snowden started whistling, "We've Got the Whole World in Our Hands." Snowden was not a religious young man, but he was spiritual. He whistled with the belief that as a team they could do anything. He felt the song gave them the glue.

Cal Snowden played for Roosevelt High School in Washington, DC, and along with his proud family sorted through a hundred scholarship offers. He chose Ohio State, but Woody Hayes said he was too soft to play defensive end. Out of high school he weighed 190 pounds, and if he hadn't gained any weight Woody Hayes would have been proven correct. Cal visited Purdue. Coach Jack Mollenkopf expressed an interest and invited him to come second semester of what would have been his freshman year. The war in Vietnam demanded soldiers, and Snowden did not wish to stay out of school and risk a telegram from his Washington, DC, draft board.

His friend and former high school teammate Cordell Gill, who was already playing for Indiana, enticed Snowden for a visit. Like most, he was swayed by the campus he called gorgeous and by John Pont's absolute assertions that if he came to Indiana his team would go to the Rose Bowl. He soon rose to first on the depth chart as defensive right end.

The raucous but small group of Indiana fans who made the trip to Champaign-Urbana were hoping the Hoosiers would not repeat their fumbling starts against Kentucky and Kansas. They endured cloudy skies and the threat of rain to encourage their team. They were rewarded for their cheers. Within two minutes of the kickoff, IU's Clarence Price pounced on an Illinois fumble at the Illinois 27-yard line. That was the first of three fumbles that plagued the Illini. Price played his high school football for Shortridge High School in Indianapolis, where he captained his team. The previous year, Price had been cited as an outstanding freshman. He continued to improve and earned a start at Illinois.

Cinderella Ball

Gonso took full advantage. He found Ben (Benny) Norman for a first and goal on the seven-yard line. On the next play, as Isenbarger crossed the goal line, he lost the ball. Offensive tackle Rick Spickard found it for a Hoosier touchdown. Kornowa kicked the extra point, then limped back to the bench and told Coach Mourouzis, "I got hit in the leg and I can't lift it." With only a minute and a half elapsed, it was IU 7-0. Spickard was a junior from Highland, Indiana, where he captained the football team and was voted Mr. Football. A knee injury kept him out of play for the entire 1966 campaign. That was the first touchdown of his collegiate career.

In need of a touchdown to even the score, Illinois quarterback Bob Naponic fashioned a long drive to the Indiana four-yard line. But a fourth-down pass was dropped, and Indiana took over with poor field position. Isenbarger knocked Illinois on its heels with a 65-yard quick kick on third down. The quarter was scoreless the rest of the way.

Twenty-seven seconds into the second quarter, Illinois quarterback Naponic faded back to throw a pass. He scrambled away from IU's rushing defensive line into the open field. Pankratz came up to make the tackle. Naponic tried to juke him but Pankratz stayed with him. As Naponic cut hard once again to avoid a tackle, his knee buckled and down he went, lost for the rest of the game. Minutes later his replacement, Bob Best, suffered a concussion. Illinois was faced with trying to beat Indiana with third-string quarterback Dean Volkman. For the rest of the first half, IU tried to give them that chance, but Illinois was unable to capitalize on IU's sloppy play, which included a fumble and a personal foul penalty. With eighteen seconds left in the half, Gonso found Butcher for the Hoosiers' second touchdown. Butcher stared over at the Illinois sidelines and held the football high over his head. With Kornowa on the bench nursing his right leg, Warner missed the extra point. Hoosiers 13-0.

In the third quarter no points were scored, and it looked like Pont's team would pull out another victory. Gonso sensed the game was won and let the Illinois defense know. Ray

Marquette of the *Indianapolis Star* said that after the Kansas game Indiana lost its bashfulness. Gonso lost his bashfulness the first time he climbed out of the crib. Offensive lineman Gary Cassells faced one of the best defensive guards in the Big Ten, Second Team All-American Fritz Harms, and Harry was agitating him. Harms was also a Big Ten weight-lifting champ and had been giving Cassells fits. Gonso said, "Hey, Fritz, see if you can catch me on this play." Fritz responded by whacking Cassells while trying to run him over. Gonso did not let up. After a particularly vicious episode, Mauro ("Monk") told Gonso in the huddle, "Shut up. Just call the play and run the play. Quit talking to their defensive linemen or we're all going to drop down and let them kill you." Fellow lineman Bob Russell, known as Bull, nodded his approval. Monk assisted his friend Cassells and together they were able to neutralize Harms—most of the time.

Early in the fourth quarter, Isenbarger attempted another quick kick on third down from his own five-yard line. Fritz Harms, still in a high state of agitation, forced Isenbarger to kick it short and high. The fair catch was fumbled, but a penalty called the play back. A quick kick is employed as a surprise play that allows the kicking team to send the football over the heads of the defensive team and eliminate any chance of a runback. Unaccountably, Isenbarger attempted a quick kick on the next play. On this third quick kick of the afternoon— the second in a row—no one was surprised. The ball was blocked into the end zone and recovered by Illinois for their first touchdown. Indiana 13, Illinois 7. Neither Pont nor Gonso owned up to calling that play, a gift to the University of Illinois.

With renewed spirit, Illinois again drove into Hoosier territory, but they lost a fumble to Sniadecki after a Brown Marks tackle on the Hoosier 30-yard line. IU failed to take advantage of the fumble recovery and gave the football back on an Isenbarger kick deep into Illinois territory. With less than three minutes left in the game, Illinois needed a touchdown to win. They went to the air. Third-string quarterback Dean

Volkman threw to a receiver running a curling pattern, but Kaczmarek stepped in front of him for an interception. Kaz, one of the Hoosiers' speediest linebackers, beat the Illinois team to the goal line for a 26-yard touchdown run. No one ever saw Kaczmarek run that fast. An Illinois player knocked him down in the end zone. Jerry Grecco ran from the sidelines to defend him, but Kaz had jumped up and thrown the ball to a sea of red in the stands. Kaz was knocked down again—this time by a joyous John Pont and forty members of the team, who piled on in a congratulatory scrum. Kaz could feel the rough stubble of Pont's beard against his neck (Pont never shaved before a game). Don Warner kicked the extra point. The game ended Indiana 20, Illinois 7.

It was the first IU team since 1928 to win its first three games, and they pulled this one off by achieving only 12 first downs compared to 22 for Illinois and scoring from the linebacker and tackle positions on two of the three touchdowns.

On the bus ride home, Pont studied the statistics. Cunningham from Danville, Illinois, had been anxious to have a good game in front of his hometown fans. He did that with sure-handed tackles and no errors. Pont decided to award Nate a game ball. Pont turned his attention to Doug Crusan's stat line. He knew Crusan and the defensive unit did not allow a touchdown, but he was astounded when he totaled the numbers. Crusan had ten tackles. Pont leaned back and sighed. Crusan had made the transition, and the IU defense was likely to be close to impenetrable for the rest of the season. John Wright of Illinois had only one reception for 14 yards until late in the fourth quarter, and no touchdowns. Pont glanced over at Kaczmarek and laughed. He was also awarded a game ball.

Pont looked at John Isenbarger's stats. His rushing and passing were credible but not what Pont had hoped from one of the best athletes on the field. Pont knew why. Isenbarger had not completed the transition from quarterback to tailback. He was comfortable handing off the ball, not getting it, and he was standing around too long watching Gonso. When he finally did have the ball, he was slow getting to the holes, and they began to close before he reached them. He wasn't using his speed and those powerful long legs to best advantage. Pont made a note for his backfield coaches to work on that in practice.

In the back of the bus, out of earshot of Coach Pont, a confidential conversation took place between Karl Pankratz and Cordell Gill. Pankratz's dogged pursuit of Illinois starting quarterback Naponic was the turning point of the game, and he was pleased with his effort, but after starting the first two games, he had been dropped to the second team in favor of Kevin Duffy for the Illinois game. Pankratz was upset. He confided in Gill, "When we came back in the fall I was still first string and as you know, I started the Kentucky and Kansas games. I had my knee taped pretty good for every practice and every game and I am a bit slower getting to the perimeter. By the end of the Kansas game it was obvious to the coaches that I lost some of my speed getting to the outside where I needed to be effective as a linebacker—and Duffy is fast."

In the midst of Pankratz's lament, Gill's interruption caught him off guard. Gill, a senior, said, "I was playing linebacker when I was a sophomore, the only sophomore to start besides Kaz (Kaczmarek) and Doug (Crusan), and I led the team in tackles. Pont then moved me to defensive tackle. I led the defensive linemen in tackles as a junior and made honorable mention All–Big Ten. Now they've moved me to defensive end. They keep moving me some place where I can't start."

Al Gage overheard part of the conversation, leaned over, and whispered to Gill and Pankratz, "Cordell has a point. You are a tremendous player Cordell. I know you love football and in each position you've played you've played well. You deserve to start somewhere on this team. Perhaps it's because you are under 5'10" and that presents situations that are difficult to overcome in a sport where you face opponents who are as tall as 6'5". Gill replied, "Although I get plenty of playing time, starts are few and far between. My response is to keep working. I was raised that if they say you are not good enough, you need to keep working until you prove to them that you are good enough."

Cal Snowden had gripes of his own, mainly with head athletic trainer Warren Ariail, who was raised in South Carolina. According to Snowden, an African American, the lens that Ariail looked through was honed through his life experiences, which didn't tell him to see blacks as equals. Ariail was a decorated Marine who fought on Tarawa in the Pacific theater in World War II. He had a Marine Corps insignia tattooed on his forearm, which he covered with a long-sleeve shirt. Ariail was respected by his mentee Dean Kleinschmidt, team members, and Big Ten trainers for providing professional care to every athlete in his charge. He was known as "the Iceman" because while the general practice was to use heat on an injury, he was the first trainer at Indiana to rely on ice in lieu of heat.

Ariail had his detractors, including Snowden; Morris (Blondie) Levy, who bore the brunt of Ariail's anti-Semitic remarks; and Duffy, who called him a battle-hardened nut case who should never be allowed on a college campus. Ariail treated Duffy for a foot injury by prescribing two morphine pills daily for a week. Duffy swallowed the pills until team doctor Brad Bomba, who in his playing days was IU's first Academic All-American, confronted him at the drinking fountain and confiscated his morphine. Bomba shot up Duffy's foot before a game with two big vials of Novocain. He drained the first vial in Duffy's ankle, then unscrewed the container, filled it up, and pumped it again. Duffy felt no pain, but when the drug wore off Duffy hobbled. Bomba treated Dave Kornowa and others in a similar manner.

The Ariail and Snowden encounter was a virulent culture clash. Snowden, from a middle-class urban family in Washington, DC, was a bright, thoughtful kid who enjoyed hitting the books as much as hitting ball carriers. On the table getting taped, he was Ariail's captive. Ariail often took the opportunity to chastise Snowden for dating Caucasians and questioned whether that would have an adverse effect on his ability to play in the pros. Snowden told Ariail that professional scouts would not be interested in who he dated. They would confine their analysis to his ability to rush a quarterback and stop a running play.

Pont had been willing to overlook Ariail's personality deficiencies and idiosyncrasies. The Iceman fixed his players, regardless of color, and got them back on the field ready to play. Pont had not been aware of Ariail's overt bigotry. Snowden was not the only black player to resent Ariail. Many remained silent, but the era of suffering those perceived and real insults in silence was rapidly coming to an end.

Across the aisle from Pont sat Bob Russell and Harry Gonso. In the gathering darkness and the serenity that comes after a hard-fought battle, Russell turned to Gonso and said, "Baby Bull, you know what? I think we're for real." Gonso had great respect for Russell, his senior by three years. The confidence expressed by Russell meant a lot to the sophomore quarterback. He said, "Thanks Bull," and started thinking about next week's battle with Iowa.

CHAPTER 7

IOWA

Brown Marks, Jim Sniadecki, and Kevin Duffy had a tradition of watching *Star Trek* in the lounge at McCormick's Creek State Park since the series began in 1966. They were devoted not only because of the creative science fiction but also because of the show's racial inclusiveness, especially Uhura, played by Nichelle Nichols, one of the few black female actors on television. A female reporter wrote about the three Trekkies after interviewing the team about its winning season. Shortly thereafter, each of them received an official certificate for their Star Trek First Officer Commission in Star Trek Command.

As a premed student, Bob Russell used his free time at McCormick's Creek to study biology and chemistry. After the past two years anchoring the offensive line for one of the most oft-beaten teams in the Big Ten, Russell was content to be playing for an undefeated team—content but not satisfied. Indiana was 3-0 and earlier in the week had broken into the UPI coaches' poll, ranked eighteenth. Russell figured, "We have a good start. Why not run the table?"

In the previous three seasons, Iowa had won two Big Ten games, both against IU. Iowa in 1967 was essentially the same

Cinderella Ball

team that edged Indiana the previous year 20-19. The near capacity crowd at Memorial Stadium was in full roar, eagerly assembled for Dad's Day and the chance to watch the newly named "Cardiac Kids" find another way to win. Gonso had tossed a touchdown pass and Butcher had caught a touchdown pass in each of the first three games. IU partisans came to see more exciting plays from IU's prodigious sophomores. Collins commented about the near capacity crowd, "In years past Indiana-Iowa games at Bloomington didn't draw enough people to start a good poker game."

The Hawkeyes, after beating Texas Christian in their first game, were knocked out early in the next two games, which they lost by a total of 96 points. The previous week, Iowa had lost to Notre Dame 56-6. It appeared that Russell and his colleagues on the offensive line would be blocking a porous opponent.

The team came out flat. Gonso threw his first career interception, an overthrow to left end Benny Norman. On IU's next series, a Gonso fumble gave Iowa an opportunity to convert a field goal from the IU 20-yard line. It was 3-0 Iowa.

Gonso settled in on the third IU series, highlighted by his run of 47 yards on an option play down to the Iowa 21-yard line. A holding call four plays later penalized Iowa to their own one-yard line, first down and goal. Center Mauro set the huddle. Monk extended his arms in field goal position, parallel just above his shoulders. Gonso entered the huddle last, opposite Mauro. Everyone leaned in with their heads down to hear exactly what the quarterback would call.

Gonso said, "Ok I-Pro-screen-left on two."

In unison, Mauro, Cassells, and Russell popped their heads up and said, "Harry, what are you doing? We can't run a play like that down here?"

Gonso repeated with emphasis, "I'm the quarterback and call the plays and it's I-Pro-screen-left on two. Ready? Break."

The play didn't go so well. As Gonso dropped back and continued to backpedal, he noticed that there was no formation of the normal distances one would see on a screen play given the tight quarters. His senior linemen were right. Harry was chased down in his own backfield and finally lost two yards on a frantic pitch to Isenbarger. Upon entering the huddle for the next play Mauro said, "Told you so." Cassells added in jest, "Your tackles will call the rest of the plays from here." Gonso understood. He called a simple pass play to Butcher who caught it in the end zone. 7-3 Indiana. As Gonso trotted off the field, Pont tapped him on the shoulder and said with a grin, "That I-Pro-screen was a pissant call."

Isenbarger's kicking game kept Iowa in check for the remainder of the first quarter. On the second play of the second quarter, IU took advantage of a flaw in the Iowa defense. Pont, an astute analyst of game films, noticed that the Iowa offensive linemen rushed the kicker until they determined that he hadn't botched the snap. They did not attempt to block the kick but rather turned abruptly around in unison like circus elephants and lumbered downfield to set up a runback for their return specialists. For a kicker, Isenbarger was a special asset. He could run with the elite in the Big Ten. All week during practice, the team ran the fake punt. It worked. Isenbarger made a show of warming up his kicking leg. He took the snap and waited for the Iowa linemen to turn, then he simply followed them down the field. The play netted 17 yards and kept an IU rally going. Isenbarger was jubilant.

Gonso had suffered from the flu all week and was flagging. While he rested and caught his breath, Mike (Redbird) Perry took charge late in the first half. A pass interference on a Perry pass brought the ball to the Iowa 16-yard line. A few plays later Indiana scored a second touchdown with Mike Krivoshia making the final carry. It was 14-3 Indiana at halftime.

An IU lapse contributed to a second half kickoff return of 40 yards, which set up an Iowa touchdown that cut the IU lead to 14-10. At the end of the third quarter, Iowa quarterback Ed Podolak, in the midst of a solid drive from the Hawkeyes' own five-yard line to past midfield, faded back for a pass and ran into the referee. The ensuing melee caused him to fumble the ball into the hands of Brown Marks. In the fourth quarter and with IU protecting a four-point lead, Isenbarger tried the fourth down fake punt once again—this time on his own. Iowa was not fooled. He needed 15 yards for a first down and fell short by 14 yards, flattened by an Iowa tackler who had been knocked down but got up in time to make the play. Pont directed a threatening finger at Isenbarger and pointed him to the end of the bench. Iowa took over on their 47-yard line and in seven plays scored the go-ahead touchdown, making the score 17-14 Iowa with 3:48 to play. Coach Nick Mourouzis, who proudly took credit for Isenbarger's booming punts, accepted no responsibility for Isenbarger's failure to punt.

It appeared Isenbarger had given away the game. Indiana had one more chance with the ball. On first down, the fans rose to their feet and cheered. Pont surveyed the full-throated IU partisans and commented to no one in particular, "This would not have happened last year." Indiana barreled its way down the field as precious minutes ticked off the clock, but they stuck at the Hawkeye 22-yard line on fourth down with twelve yards needed to earn four more downs. The team could try a field goal, which would tie the game, or they could attempt a touchdown play, probably a pass for the win. Pont called timeout. Gonso ran to the sidelines and said to Coach Pont, "What do you want us to do? Kick or do the fake?" Pont replied, "What do you think?" As play resumed with little more than a minute left on the clock, Pont sent in his placekicker Donny Warner to kick the game-tying field goal. Gonso knelt a few yards behind the line to take the snap and hold the ball for the kick attempt. Almost fifty thousand people were sure the Hoosiers were attempting to salvage a tie, but as soon as Gonso gathered in the ball, he held it in the air above the kicking tee. As Warner proceeded with his kicking motion, Gonso pulled the ball to his stomach and sprinted around left end toward the goal line. He fell four yards short of a touchdown but ran far enough to earn a first down.

With less than a minute left in the game, Gonso called a pass play down the right sideline to Butcher. Gonso noted the Iowa defensive halfback was just behind Butcher in close coverage. Gonso ran to his right, hounded by would-be tacklers. He motioned with his left hand for Butcher to sprint to the middle. The defense was caught out of position. As Gonso was about to be tackled, he passed to Butcher for the winning touchdown. Gonso witnessed the score from flat on his back, prompting Collins to quip, "Gonso attacks the game of football with the dexterity of an apprentice juggler on a raft in a hurricane." The final score was Indiana 21, Iowa 17. At the postgame press conference Pont deadpanned, "Ties don't seem to settle with me."

Collins said, "The last time Indiana was 4-0 wasn't revealed until just recently when the school received the latest translation of the Dead Sea Scrolls." In fact it was 1910. Collins added, "This game had more twists than a go-go dancer," and he followed with, "The Hoosiers have not found four teams they could beat at the start of any season since back in the days when that pigskin was made out of the skin of a pig."

Al Grady, columnist for the *Iowa City Press-Citizen*, wrote in his column, "The Hawkeyes had Indiana's miracle Hoosiers beaten and let 'em off the hook—fooled by a fake field goal play which is older than the pyramids." He ended his column with an observation: "It used to be that you were afraid to wade into Big Ten competition after beating your non-conference foes, but Iowa found Saturday that the Big Ten is exactly where it belongs. The Hawkeyes may not be very good but neither is Indiana. Let's not kid ourselves, Indiana is not a great football team. It is not even a very good one but it IS unbeaten, which beats being three or four times beaten."

Max Stultz, *Star* sportswriter, called the Iowa game a "Flim-Flam Job." Iowa coach Nagel said the game was "the most crushing and heart-breaking in my ten years as a coach."

Bill and Jane Orwig threw a party. Jane cooked her famous chicken and rice dish for a hundred guests who wouldn't leave Pont alone, all talking about how he stole one from the Hawkeyes. In light of the magic ending, everyone was too ecstatic to be bothered by Isenbarger's antics. Everyone but John Pont.

    Late that night as the euphoria of the Iowa victory began to fade, Pont blamed himself for designating Isenbarger as his punter. Although he could clearly move the ball as far as anybody in the Big Ten, the less mercurial Terry Cole, the previous year's punter, had finished 1966 as the second best punter in the Big Ten. Nobody could kick like John Isenbarger. For that matter, nobody could triple threat like John Isenbarger. He could run, pass, and kick. Pont leaned back and laughed. He thought about what he had overheard when half the stadium stormed the field, "Well, Isenbarger is a quadruple threat. He can run, pass, kick, and fail to kick." Michigan was on tap for Saturday. Pont wondered what would Isenbarger do next—or fail to do.

Cinderella Ball

Isenbarger (17) punts against Kansas.

Gonso (16) on a keeper against Wisconsin.

Cinderella Ball

A team effort against Purdue: Applegate (53), Perry (18), Krivoshia (35), Russell (64), Cassells (68).

Mike Krivoshia

Cinderella Ball

Terry Cole

Jade Butcher

CHAPTER 8

MICHIGAN

Bill and Jane Orwig traveled with their son, Bill Orwig Jr., to Ann Arbor for the contest with Michigan. They stayed with the IU contingent even though Orwig's daughter and other family members lived in Ann Arbor. The night before the game, Orwig attended a party at the home of his friend, Don Canham, the Michigan athletic director, where he met many of his old pals and shared stories of past glories. It was clear to all that Orwig had been won over. He was an Indiana man, a Hoosier. A number of friendly wagers were made. Oddsmakers installed Michigan as a three-point favorite. Orwig took the points.

The crowd filling the cavernous Michigan Stadium in Ann Arbor on October 21 was unofficially the largest to witness an Indiana football game in 1967. The official estimate was 65,800 but that undercounted students who streamed into the stadium all morning without tickets, without seat assignments, and without resistance. The student section stood the entire game, which allowed double-packed student fans to stand on what would have been a seat. The roar of 65,800 fans sounded more like 70,000 fans because 70,000 was closer to the actual attendance.

The relatively few loyal Hoosier fans who made the trip were introduced to a Michigan ritual: as each starting IU player was introduced, voices rose with the rejoinder, "Who cares?" Unique to Michigan Stadium and sanctioned by the university was the policy of "no women or children allowed on the field."

Thunderous drumbeats signaled the appearance of the Michigan marching band. Michigan partisans not already standing rose to sing "Hail to the Victors," first performed by John Philip Sousa and widely considered the most stirring fight song in the Big Ten:

Hail! To the victors valiant
Hail! To the conqu'ring heroes
Hail! Hail! to Michigan
The leaders and best

In the rousing spirit of college football, the band always belted out "Hail to the Victors" following every Michigan score. In contrast, Collins wrote in the *Star*, "Indiana has been known for a million years as a day off for title contenders." He added, "Even the school fight song seems to compliment the team. Compared to other school marches it sounds like a waltz."

The Michigan football tradition dated back to the early 1900s. At one time the program boasted a fifty-five-game winning streak. In 1967, however, a depleted Michigan team limped into this game with a 1-3 record, which included a 34-0 shellacking by cross-state rival Michigan State and not a single victory over a Big Ten opponent. The team had graduated fourteen starters from the previous year. Nonetheless, no one in Michigan was cowed by Indiana's undefeated record, including the oddsmakers. Bob Hoerner, sportswriter for the *Lansing State Journal*, pointed out that Indiana's four victims had won only three games while losing thirteen. He sided with the oddsmakers and picked Michigan and its All-American candidate, fullback Ron Johnson, over Indiana. Even Jack Berry of the *Detroit Free Press*, in sizing up probable Rose Bowl Big Ten representatives, chose to disregard Indiana's unbeaten record and called it a tossup between Michigan State and Minnesota. Historians will be hard pressed to find another situation in which a 4-0 record was rated below a 1-3 record in the same league.

In the locker room before the game, the defense was in a foul mood. Coach Plank made them practice all week in ugly, shit brown uniforms to remind them how poorly they had played against Iowa. Pont urged the team to disregard odds, favorites, or homecoming celebrations. Athletic departments up and down the Big Ten endeavored to schedule a "patsy" for their homecoming matchup, and Indiana was always high on the list. Michigan snagged IU for 1967 homecoming expecting another walkover. By game time they knew IU was not going to be the homecoming guest they had come to expect.

Before game time coach Bump Elliott, in an effort to jump-start his team, announced that junior quarterback Dennis Brown had earned a start. Brown was a scrambling quarterback who had proved himself earlier in the season against Michigan State, picking up 62 yards in the second half. Brown could also throw the ball. Elliott made additional changes on the defensive and offensive side of the line.

Indiana, with a chance to go 5-0 for the first time since the invention of sliced bread, took a punt on their 23-yard line and scored on their first series. Isenbarger set up the score with a pass to Butcher on the option play that had been difficult to defend all season. A few plays later Isenbarger pranced 26 yards down the east sideline for the score. The run appeared easy only because offensive lineman Bob Russell went through the line from his right guard position as Isenbarger swept the left end. He used his speed to get ahead of the play and then peeled back to screen off four potential tacklers who were closing in on Isenbarger. Russell, a brilliant, soft-spoken senior, quipped after the game, "Keeping up with Harry is the hardest part of the job. We just keep blocking until the ball flies over our heads or all of a sudden Harry goes running by." Warner kicked the extra point. On Michigan's next series, All-American candidate

Ron Johnson took a pitchout from Dennis Brown and ran into the arms of hard-hitting Nate Cunningham. The ball popped out and was pounced on by Doug Crusan. A seven-yard Gonso-to-Stolberg pass sewed up the second touchdown, and the first quarter ended 14-0.

In the second quarter, Nate Cunningham recovered the Wolverines' third fumble at their 41-yard line. Isenbarger took a pitch back from Gonso and promptly lofted a pass to Butcher standing all alone in the end zone. The extra point was missed. Before the students finished their second beer, Michigan was losing 20-0. "Hail to the Victors" had not been heard since before the opening kickoff. Michigan fans didn't wait for halftime to file out of the stadium. Other homecoming activities began for them earlier than planned. Just before halftime, Michigan's Tom Curtis recovered a fumble that led to a score, making it 20-7 at the break.

Indiana still had not figured out how to win easy. On the first play from scrimmage in the third quarter, Isenbarger threw an interception to Curtis. Michigan accepted the favor and drove 55 yards in eight plays, aided by two IU consecutive offsides penalties, and scored to close the gap to 20-14. The Wolverines were only one touchdown away from the lead, and Isenbarger was about to give it to them.

For the rest of the third quarter, a series of possessions yielded no score. Notable was an Isenbarger punt that rolled out of bounds on the Michigan two-yard line. The third quarter ended with Michigan in possession of the ball and Indiana holding on to that one-touchdown lead.

As the fourth quarter began, the temperature hit its high for the day of 50 degrees. The Wolverines moved the ball 28 yards and ten plays but were held on downs. Indiana took possession on their own five-yard line but failed to move the ball and were forced to punt. Incredibly, Isenbarger decided to run on fourth down and fumbled the ball on the IU 16-yard line. Pont flung his headphones thirty yards down the sidelines. As Isenbarger walked off the field, Kaczmarek said to him, "Iso, what in the hell are you doing? Just punt the damn ball."

Michigan

Before Pont could say a word, Isenbarger rushed up to him with his hands on his headgear and yelled, "Coach, why do I do things like that?" Pont put his face in the grill of Isenbarger's facemask and whispered, "Get your ass on the end of that bench. You're through." Dennis Brown immediately dashed 12 yards on a quarterback delay to the four-yard line. An interference penalty moved the ball half the distance to the goal line. Brown drove to the one-yard line, and Ron Johnson took a handoff from Brown and dove the last yard into the end zone. A bad pass from center spoiled the conversion try. What was initially a 20-0 rout was now a 20-20 tie.

Moments later Krivoshia fumbled at the IU 28-yard line and Michigan drove to the five-yard line. On third down and one yard to go for a first down, the give was to Johnson, who made many of his yards on second effort. He took the handoff and appeared to be stopped, but as he summoned his second effort to break through for the first down, Kaczmarek hit him straight up and knocked him back. Michigan elected to try a field goal on fourth down, but the 22-yard attempt was wide to the left.

The Hoosiers took over on their own 20-yard line with little more than ten minutes to play. Gonso immediately incurred a five-yard penalty for delay of the game. Gonso called timeout, trotted over to Pont, and said, "Coach if we're going to win this game I have to have Isenbarger. I need this guy. If you must, punish him later." They both glanced over at Isenbarger sitting on the end of the bench as instructed. His helmet was off and his head was between his knees. Pont signaled to his quadruple threat to take the field. Isenbarger accepted the invitation, according to Collins, like a fellow who would rather die on the field than be strangled by his coach. With the starting backfield intact, the team began its march.

Isenbarger wasted no time. He swept around left end for eight yards. After Gonso passed to Butcher for 12 yards, Isenbarger took the ball again for a yard. Gonso passed to Gage right up the middle for 31 more. Isenbarger ran off ten yards and then six more. Cole went off right guard for four;

Isenbarger took a pitch and ran for eight and then ran for four more. Cole tried the center for no gain, and Isenbarger took the last yard for a touchdown with less than two minutes on the clock. Gonso held for the extra point and Warner converted. Michigan's desperate attempt to tie the score was abruptly ended on a Kornowa interception at the Indiana 22-yard line.

At the final whistle, Bill Orwig sprinted to the locker room to congratulate the coaching staff and team, and they tossed him into the shower. As he toweled off, Pont presented him the game ball with the score written on it: Indiana 27–Michigan 20. Orwig cherished that ball and the IU victory over Michigan.

According to Bob Collins, Isenbarger went from goat to hero by scoring the winning touchdown, and he saved himself from a new Indiana record—being the first Hoosier football player ever to walk home from Ann Arbor. After the game Isenbarger went up to Coach Pont and said, "Coach, what are you going to do about me?" Pont laughed, "How do you answer that one?"

Michigan coach Bump Elliott praised Indiana but was not effusive. He told the Chicago Football Writers, "Indiana is a quick team with the wide open option. They strike quickly and hurt you. I won't say they are the best in the conference, but they keep coming up with what it takes to win, week after week, and any team that can do that has to be considered a strong contender." Bob Collins, *Indianapolis Star* sports editor, summed up the game, "The 1967 football team discovered yesterday afternoon that they can't even beat themselves in spite of the fact that they frittered away a twenty to nothing lead and waited until 1:10 showed on the clock before coming back to whip Michigan 27-20." He said that this is the first time Indiana has been 5-0 at the start of any season since George Rogers Clark shut out the Indians at Vincennes. Pont agreed. He told the press, "If we can put together a complete game it's going to be a lot easier on the coaching staff, even though the fans may not like it as well." Pont flashed a wide grin.

After church on Sunday, Pont was in his office as usual to review the prior game and plan for the week ahead and IU's next opponent. Halfway through the season, IU was the only unbeaten team in the Big Ten, winning all five games by a puny total of 29 points. His thoughts continued to drift back to Isenbarger. Pont concluded it was Isenbarger's intense desire to keep the offense on the field that led him to unwarranted, crazy risks. Pont thought that Isenbarger had finally learned a lesson and would follow directions—for the most part—the rest of the season. The one thing Isenbarger did not want to do was sit the bench. Isenbarger's performance was remarkable. He was the team's leading ground gainer with 101 yards in 18 tries. He had completed two of three passes for 79 yards, scored two touchdowns, passed for another, kicked four punts an average of 36.7 yards, and failed to kick one punt. Isenbarger had completed the transition.

Pont turned his attention to some of the other performances. Stolberg caught a touchdown pass. He played through pain, marking time until off-season surgery to shorten and retie ligaments that would hold his shoulder in place. The harness was working to prevent his shoulder from popping out, but it restricted his reach. His speed and sure hands erased that deficiency. Pont jotted a letter to Stolberg's mother, Bernice, congratulating her on her son's performance and bringing her up to date on a number of other items he knew would be of interest. Correspondence with Bernice had begun when Stolberg arrived at IU. Stolberg had lost his father in an automobile accident when he was a senior in high school, and Bernice was concerned about her son's adjustment. Pont hatched this arrangement. Stolberg never knew.

Pont checked on the Crusan stat line. Before the game, Crusan sought out Pont for a discussion about going back to offense. Crusan recovered two fumbles and made ten tackles, six of which were solos. Pont awarded him a game ball, and he was also named Midwest Lineman of the Week for those efforts. He checked the stat sheet on his starting linebackers and noted they were responsible for 45 tackles, 24 of which were solos. According to the defensive plan, they keyed on Ron

Johnson and held him to 28 net yards, but quarterback Dennis Brown surprised them with his quickness and speed. He burned IU for 127 yards, running the option plays. It was a fair trade-off to bottling up the elusive Johnson.

Arizona was his next opponent. The Wildcats had beaten Ohio State and were disrespectful in the press toward the Big Ten. Pont was sure he would win in Tucson. He had uncovered a little secret.

CHAPTER 9
ARIZONA

Indiana represented the Big Ten in Arizona from the top of the conference, tied for first place with Minnesota and Purdue. None of those teams had lost a Big Ten game. Bob Collins wrote on Monday after the victory at Michigan, "The 1967 Indiana football team is the most exciting thing to hit the Bloomington campus since publication of the Kinsey Report." The Hoosiers brought their gaudy league best 5-0 record to Tucson expecting respect from Arizona. They didn't get it.

Earlier in the season, the Wildcats posted a 14-7 victory over Ohio State in Columbus. Pont pored over a tape of that game and concluded Ohio State was not the best the Big Ten had to offer in 1967. Ohio State had difficulty scoring against a defensive front four that averaged 236 pounds and linebackers almost as big. And no one was going to outleap Ed Caruthers, the Arizona safety who was one of the world's greatest high jumpers with an elite mark of 7'2¼". However, Pont did spot a weakness—in poker parlance, a tic.

It was the first night game of the season for IU: 8:00 p.m. local time. The temperature had hovered in the mid-eighties all day but dropped by game time to a "cool" seventy-five degrees.

The IU team drank water and Gatorade all day to avoid dehydration while they enjoyed the respite from the Midwest autumn and that nippy air in Michigan the week before.

More than a few Hoosier fans in their red berets were dispersed throughout the stadium, but they were difficult to discern in the sea of Arizona red and blue. The largest out-of-state press contingent to cover an Arizona home game was on hand. Seven newspapers (*Chicago Tribune, Bloomington Herald-Telephone, Bloomington Tribune, Indianapolis Star, Indianapolis News, Courier-Journal, and Fort Wayne Journal-Gazette*) and two radio stations followed the unbeaten Indiana team's first ever meeting with the Arizona Wildcats.

An hour before the game, Karl Pankratz went into the training room for Ariail to tape his knee. He found offensive lineman Gary Cassells sitting on the table in considerable discomfort. While Dave Kornowa awaited his turn, Ariail injected Cassells's shoulder using a needle that looked to be a foot long, which he moved all around the affected area. Pankratz felt the pain. Cassells had played hurt all year.

In an interview for the *Tucson Daily Citizen*, Arizona coach Darrell Mudra, known for having "the gift of jab," summed up his opinion of the Indiana record and its schedule: "I don't care if we are six point underdogs. Indiana is not a very good football team. We can beat them. We play in a better conference than they do." Pont received fifteen copies of the story via airmail from former Indiana residents living in Arizona. Pont reacted as though someone had slapped his daughter. His locker room pregame show reached a crescendo. With a toss of his red thermos, coffee splattered the walls of the visitor's locker room. Everyone heard as he spoke just above a whisper, "They are trying to hurt our pride. The honor of IU and the Big Ten conference is at stake. Tonight we are going to make a statement."

And a statement they made. The first two times IU had the ball, they scored with their typical series of sweeps and options, all in the first two minutes and 48 seconds. The first touchdown was set up by a Gonso pass to Butcher for 38 yards and the second by a Gonso 49-yard romp around right end, a costly romp. Gonso stayed in long enough to complete his business, a one-yard keeper for a touchdown, then left the game with a deep right shoulder bruise. He spent the rest of the evening pacing the sidelines. He had played only six minutes.

Enter Mike Perry. In short order, Redbird executed the option pass to Butcher via a pitch to Isenbarger for another touchdown. That ran the score up to 19-0.

Arizona's only score in the first half was made possible by a block of an Isenbarger punt. The Indiana faithful were only slightly disappointed with the Arizona score, taking great pains to point out that at least Isenbarger did not attempt a run from punt formation. Before the game Pont had read the team a telegram Isenbarger received from his mother. She closed her message to her son with, "P.S. listen to Coach Pont and punt."

At halftime in the Arizona locker room, Coach Mudra exhorted Marc Reed, his quarterback, to move the ball. Reed replied, "Coach they seem to anticipate our every move." There was an explanation for that.

As the second half opened, Terry Cole dragged tacklers into the end zone for a touchdown. Perry ran in the two-point attempt, making the score 27-7. On the last play of the third quarter, defensive back Nate Cunningham added to the scoring barrage when he intercepted an Arizona pass and returned it 41 yards for a touchdown. Giving up on Warner, who had had two extra points blocked, Perry ran it in a second time for an Indiana lead of 35-7.

Midway through the fourth quarter, Perry found Butcher for a 73-yard touchdown pass play. Butcher turned and ran the last 20 yards with the ball held high in one hand like a runner ending an Olympic torch run, a stick in the eye of Coach Mudra. The game mercifully ended for Arizona with the final score Indiana 42, Arizona 7. It could have been more. Butcher returned a punt 61 yards for a touchdown that was called back on a clipping call that took place at least ten yards behind him. Blondie was working the press booth during the game, where decorum rivals that of a public library. After the team scored 42 points he yelled, "Go for fifty! Go for fifty!" His enthusiasm was not appreciated. IU already had 435 yards of offense.

Pont told Perry, "We're not going to run up the score" and gave extra minutes to many players lower in the depth chart, including Al Schmidt, Steve Applegate, Jay Mathias, and Mike Deal. It was the only blowout win of the season. According to Dave Spriggs, sportswriter for the *Tucson Daily Citizen*, "The option pass came off so well for Indiana that Arizona's deep secondary was usually nowhere near the receiver. On one play the secondary was beaten so badly that when the field announcer stated, '(Doug) Schleuter defending on the play,' it drew as big a laugh as a Henny Youngman one-liner." In Pont's postgame comments he said, "Arizona's tremendous size caused us a lot of concern so we decided to try and go outside of them. We out-quicked Arizona in this manner."

Pont awarded the game ball to senior defensive halfback Kornowa. He also cited others for their extraordinary efforts. Butcher scored two touchdowns with five receptions and gained 170 yards. Mike Perry, off the bench, led the team with five completions in seven tries for 157 yards and his first collegiate touchdown. It was said after the game that there was more than one capable quarterback wearing the red and white, and that would be true. Perry had excelled in football, basketball, and track for Broad Ripple High School in Indianapolis. During his high school career he played safety, running back, tight end, wide receiver, and quarterback. Redbird was recruited by a few schools including Purdue. He could have started at quarterback for many Big Ten teams.

After the game, the team carried Pont off to the dressing room while singing "He's Got the Whole World in His Hands." Spriggs wrote, "The harmony wasn't quite as crisp as their play execution but the lyrics exemplified the tenor of their mood."

> John's got the best damn offense in his hands
> He's got the best damn defense in his hands
> He's got the Big Ten champions in his hands
> He's got the Rose Bowl in his hands.

Arizona guard John Matishak was asked, "Were they tough?" Gesturing toward the door, he replied, "Go outside and look at the scoreboard." Arizona coach Darrell Mudra found some gallows humor in the shellacking. He quipped, "One thing I've noticed is that since I've spent more time with the squad and have done more coaching myself, the team has gotten worse... which is disconcerting!"

Pont did not travel home with the team. He left early to meet an obligation for a television interview. On his flight he reviewed the stats of the Arizona game. Butcher's record through the Arizona game was 25 catches for 497 yards and nine touchdowns, one touchdown short of the Indiana season record established by Tom Nowatzke in 1964. He was named Midwest Lineman of the Week for his work in the Arizona game. He was also Indiana's top punt and kickoff return man and an excellent blocker. Pont reread Bansch, who had opined in the *Indianapolis Star* that Pont had produced the greatest success story of the 1967 football season. He noted that the team was now ranked tenth in the nation, only the second time in history. Pont reviewed Mike Perry's stat line. He took a 13-0 lead and made it 42-7 at the final whistle. Pont was glad he remembered to compliment Perry after the game. Cassells, although hurt, played another great game. He was tough, big, strong, and quick. Finally, he looked at his defense. The defense did not allow a single score all afternoon. There was a reason. Pont had shared his discovery with his linebackers. He had noticed from viewing the tape of the Arizona–Ohio State game that the Arizona guards led the play to where the ball carrier was going every time, whether they pulled their guards right or left or came straight ahead. Armed with that information, the IU defense keyed on the guards and was a step ahead of Arizona all day.

At his TV appearance Pont was congratulated for producing a season start unsurpassed in IU football history. When asked about the game he said, "Perry's performance showed he is an excellent runner and can pass the ball too. He had poise and was never really ruffled, even when he threw a pass after going past the line of scrimmage. Our kids were really high for this one. They were playing for the pride of the Big Ten as well as Indiana. After hearing how superior the WAC is supposed to be they wanted to prove our brand of football isn't bad." In answer to an inquiry about Isenbarger he said, "We don't know whether to raise a statue to him or shoot him." Pont wondered how he could motivate his team next week against bottom-dweller but dangerous Wisconsin.

CHAPTER 10
WISCONSIN

Halloween night found John Pont in his den trying to relax with a glass of scotch and a mystery story. It wasn't working. He was no more relaxed than when he watched a crucial down in front of fifty thousand roaring fans. Like the devil on his right shoulder, tension was always there during the season. By Tuesday, football chased all other thoughts into a corner, where they stayed until Sunday night. This Tuesday he was preoccupied with his next opponent, Wisconsin, and its league-leading tacklers Ken Criter and Tom Domres.

The doorbell chimes were a welcome distraction. Four barefoot "goblins" clad in white sheets with heads covered with jumbo carved pumpkins shouted "trick or treat." Pont's wife, Sandy, went to the door to investigate, took one look at the foursome, and called her husband to the scene.

The trick or treaters became silent, staring straight ahead through their pumpkin shells. Finally, one of the "goblins" smiled and Pont saw a retainer wire used to straighten teeth. He recognized the mouth of senior linebacker Ken (Kaz) Kaczmarek, then he realized the other two men were Kevin Duffy and Brown Marks, also senior linebackers.

The Indiana football coach invited the three players and their friend, Jane Bumb, into the house. They took off their pumpkins and sheets to enjoy Sandy's offering of soft drinks and Halloween candy. After chatting for a while, the group donned their costumes once again to make other "calls" around campus. As Brown Marks, an African American, draped his sheet over his head, he looked at Kevin Duffy and said, "Oh, if the brothers could see me now."

According to Star writer John Bansch, "The incident is a perfect example of the rapport Pont has developed with his players while bringing Indiana football standards to their highest level since the glory of 1945." Pont explained to Bansch, "While there is no funny business on the field, we don't want the players to feel the coaches are beyond reach or untouchable." Bansch concluded that the IU coach wanted his players loose mentally and he wanted them to play a wide-open game. The lack of pressure helped immensely in the fourth quarter this season as the Hoosiers had their backs to the wall in all but one of the games.

Football and Wisconsin preoccupied Pont's thoughts once again. He had a reason to be concerned. Gonso's status for the game was listed as questionable by Dr. Brad Bomba, who had examined Gonso's deep right shoulder bruise and ordered him to the infirmary when the team arrived home from Arizona.

Gonso had a different concern. Backup quarterback Mike Perry had smoothly directed the IU offense with devastating results to the Arizona Wildcats. Perry was on the field for 29 of IU's 42 points, and he felt he deserved the opportunity to start at Wisconsin in place of the injured Gonso. Gonso conceded to himself that Perry was an able backup. He was afraid that Pont would give Perry the start, at least for the Wisconsin game. On Monday evening, Gonso had phoned Coach Pont from his infirmary bed and said, "Coach, this is Harry Gonso. Remember me?"

"How could I possibly forget?" replied Pont.

On Gonso's insistence he was released from the infirmary on Tuesday, Halloween day, and he declared himself ready to play.

Dr. Bomba was not convinced. He did not release Gonso to work out until Friday. In response to inquiries from the press, Pont said, "At this point in the season one day should be enough to prepare. Gonso should be ready. We'll go with our first team."

November 4 was not a pleasant day in Bloomington. A cold fifteen-miles-per-hour wind penetrated the stadium from the northwest end zone and whipped its way across the field. By game time snow flurries covered the coats of the homecoming crowd. The closely huddled students, alumni, friends, and neighbors gathered their coats and blankets and pulled their red IU knit hats down around their ears.

Bill Orwig added bleachers to the open south end of Memorial Stadium that included 1,500 seats he sold for one dollar each to area youngsters he dubbed "knothole kids." The temporary seats increased capacity to 50,344, most of which were filled and packed in tightly, mainly to keep warm. A little wind and a few snowflakes were not going to deter the plucky IU fans who spun the turnstiles in record numbers to watch the undefeated Hoosiers walk over their "homecoming patsy," the winless Wisconsin Badgers, for their seventh straight victory. The oddsmakers agreed. Seventh-ranked Indiana, one of seven undefeated teams in the nation—the others being Dartmouth, Wyoming, UCLA, North Carolina State, Virginia Tech, and University of Southern California, was favored by fourteen points.

It was a jolly throng, animated with high expectations and finally with something to shout about—IU in a romp over Wisconsin. Dan Jenkins said in *Sports Illustrated*, "A football phenomenon has overflowed the banks of the Wabash." He added, "Indiana University had as much romance in its football past as a stone quarry."

Awaiting the kickoff, the crowd tossed little red balls handed out by the stadium staff that read "Keep the Ball Rolling." Some carried homemade signs: "John Isenbarger is Bart Maverick," "Harry Gonso Wears Elevator Shoes," and "God Would Punt." Students of the game and close followers of the IU team twitched with the anticipation that anything could happen regardless of prior performances. They were prescient.

Minutes after the game got underway, Wisconsin was forced to punt. Butcher called for a fair catch at the 45-yard line of Wisconsin, but as he tried to field the ball, Wisconsin's Mel Reddick ran into him. Referees paced the personal foul penalty to the Badgers' 30-yard line. It was the quick-strike sophomores from that point. Gonso ran for eight yards then lost three yards. After Isenbarger lost two yards, he took a pitch from Gonso and passed to Butcher for 13 yards. Isenbarger lost another yard then caught a Gonso pass for 15 yards and a touchdown. IU partisans were getting what they paid for. The quarter ended with IU ahead 7-0.

During the second quarter, the Hoosiers constantly battled bad field position, taking over at their own 3, 1, and 15-yard lines. IU punter John Isenbarger gamely matched the Badgers including a 41-yard punt on third down. Each time IU lined up in punt formation the homecoming throng arose and serenaded Isenbarger with "Punt John Punt!" It was all quite fun for everyone but Coach Pont. When asked by one of the players on the sidelines if Isenbarger was going to run or kick, Pont said, "I have no idea. Every play is a surprise around here." On one fourth down play center Harold Mauro snapped the ball over Isenbarger's head. Isenbarger turned his back and ran looking for the football in his own end zone while being chased by the entire Badger defensive unit. He scooped up the ball as Pont, desperate to prevent a Wisconsin touchdown on a fumble or blocked kick, yelled from the sideline, "John, fall on the ball." But John had been instructed to punt. He ran up and down behind his goal line until he found a narrow alleyway in which to loft a 37-yard kick through the wall of Wisconsin linemen.

Those who left the stands in the final moments of the first half to be first in line at the restrooms and the refreshment stands missed a whole game's worth of entertainment. Thirty-eight seconds before halftime, Wisconsin finally leveraged its field position and scored a 27-yard field goal. On the last play of the first half, with Indiana holding a 7-3 lead, Gonso threw an

Wisconsin

interception to Wisconsin linebacker Sam Wheeler. According to *Sports Illustrated's* Jenkins, the nearest tackler to Wheeler was in Fort Wayne. Wheeler ran 35 yards but at the IU 25, with a touchdown in his sight, one of his teammates came roaring up to him and tripped him from behind.

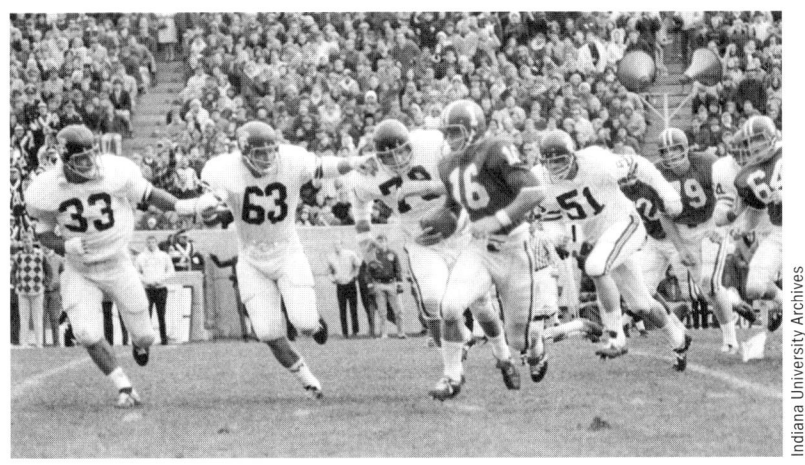

Run Harry (16) run!

Gage (81) snares a pass for a long gain in a drive that failed.

In the third quarter, Brown Marks intercepted a pass that had been tipped by Tom Bilunas on the Wisconsin 34-yard line and ran it back to their 27-yard line. Bilunas battled Clarence Price all season for one of the starting defensive end spots. Bilunas started the Kentucky game but lost to Price at Kansas and Illinois. Both players logged many snaps. Bilunas attended Andrean High School in Gary, Indiana, where he was named most valuable player on the Andrean High School team and was chosen for the all-state football team. He was recruited by Indiana and Michigan and chose Indiana on the recommendation of Andrean teammate Jerry Grecco, one year his senior. At 6'2" and a playing weight of 215 pounds, he was large for defensive end.

Gonso, while driving toward the Wisconsin goal line, fumbled the ball but the play was nullified for defensive holding. Gonso went to the bench with a wrist injury. Aided by a Wisconsin penalty, Redbird guided the team to the Wisconsin one-yard line, where Krivoshia dove across the goal line. Don Warner added the extra point. For the remainder of the third quarter, neither team could take advantage of their opponent's mistakes. Wisconsin was called for a personal foul and was immediately assessed another 15 yards for unsportsmanlike conduct from the bench. Badger linebacker John Borders was ejected from the game. Gonso blunted the IU momentum by throwing an interception at the Wisconsin 14-yard line. Wisconsin returned the favor, giving up an interception to Kevin Duffy on its 43-yard line. Both teams suffered penalties for illegal receivers downfield. The third quarter ended with the score IU 14, Wisconsin 3.

In the fourth quarter, Isenbarger punted the ball away on IU's first possession. Wisconsin took over on its 37-yard line. Wisconsin made four first downs on four successive plays and scored a touchdown on a two-yard keeper by John Boyajian after he faked to the fullback and followed him over right tackle. The two-point conversion attempt failed, and IU led 14-9. Time was running out. A Wisconsin onside kick attempt did not travel the required ten yards. The short kick gave Indiana the ball on the Wisconsin 44-yard line, but the Hoosiers could do nothing with it and called on Isenbarger to kick on fourth down. Isenbarger's worst punt of the season, a ball off the side of his foot, traveled only four yards before it went out of bounds, giving the Badgers a final opportunity to upset the Hoosiers with 2:08 on the clock. Wisconsin needed a touchdown to win. Wisconsin converted on two successive fourth-down plays and drove to the 10-yard line with only twenty ticks left. The Badgers incurred a five-yard offside penalty that moved the ball back to the 15. They got those yards back on a five-yard pass, but that left time for just one more play. Jenkins wrote that the IU defense looked about as organized as a panty raid.

Just as the ball was snapped, the gun went off, ending the game. Wisconsin's John Boyajian spotted his favorite receiver Mel Reddick in the end zone and tossed the ball in his direction. Jenkins reckoned that the ball sailed over the library, which was about a mile away. The game ended IU 14, Wisconsin 9, the first victory over the Wisconsin Badgers since 1948. The homecoming crowd practically danced out of the stadium. The next day, Star sportswriter Dave Overpeck opined, "The intoxicating scent of roses that perfumes the southern Indiana hills this fall almost turned to stink weed."

In the locker room amid the whistling, singing, and laughing, Kaz told the press corps, "Any win is a good victory. This one was not pretty but it seems that is the way we win our games." The IU game ball was awarded to Kevin Duffy for his masterful third-quarter interception and his team high 13 tackles. At Nick's, Bloomington's most popular watering hole, there were plenty of explanations to go around: the team was overconfident, buoyed by their easy victory over Arizona; the team was looking ahead to Michigan State, a more formidable opponent; Gonso played with a heavily taped right shoulder impeding his throwing motion (he was 2 of 11); Gonso didn't have time to practice; Perry should have started after all.

Someone summed it up, "Indiana has been winning 'moral' victories for years; it's about time we won an 'immoral' one." The discussion did not consider that Wisconsin's Ken Criter played a standout game. He had 16 solo tackles and recovered one Indiana fumble. At that pace he would lead the Big Ten in tackles for the second consecutive year. Kaz would finish second.

The weekend battles reduced the number of undefeated teams to four: UCLA, Virginia Tech, Dartmouth, and IU. In his postgame interview Pont commented that it was a rugged, inconsistent ballgame. He said, "We were just too tight. That's just not our style. We have to play wide open. The edge just wasn't there and it was hard to get up for an 0-5-1 team. Wisconsin is much better than their record." Then he grinned and said it's nice to smile after you've played this poorly. He didn't say much else. His mind was already on his date with Michigan State in East Lansing on Veteran's Day, November 11, and the opportunity to avenge last year's physical beating.

CHAPTER 11
MICHIGAN STATE

It was pouring in East Lansing, not ideal for Indiana's slashing and passing game. The previous week, Indiana had ducked an upset by Wisconsin but managed to nurse its record winning streak one more game. In spite of Pont's best efforts, many on the team looked past Wisconsin to the day they could renew the battle with Michigan State, and win it. On November 11, 1967, that day arrived. The team cast a vengeful eye at Michigan State. They were focused—like the US Postal Service, weather would not be a deterrent.

Michigan State University, located on the banks of the Red Cedar River just three miles east of the state capital, Lansing, had only recently acquired its shortened name. Until January 1, 1964, it was known as Michigan State University of Agriculture and Applied Science. Spartan Stadium had a seating capacity of more than 71,000 and the fans to fill it. Sparty, the mascot adorned in school colors green and white, enjoyed the run of the field.

The year before, Michigan State, unbeaten and ranked number two, participated in what many called the "Game of the Century," a battle against Notre Dame, unbeaten and ranked number one. It was the first time since the AP began polling that the number one team played the number two team. Spartan Stadium was filled with more than eighty thousand fans, well over its capacity. Tied at 10-10 late in the game, Notre Dame, with the ball at their own 30-yard line, elected to run out the clock instead of trying to move into field-goal range. Fans and foes accused Notre Dame coach Ara Parseghian of cowardice. *Sports Illustrated*'s Dan Jenkins wrote, "Parseghian chose to 'tie one for the Gipper.'" Notre Dame crushed the University of Southern California 51-0 in their next game, prompting John McKay, coach of his demoralized team, to say, "There are 800 million people in China who didn't even know this game was played." The victory over USC clinched the national title for the Irish.

Controversy was still raging in 1967. On October 25, a few days after suffering a crushing 21-0 defeat at the hands of Minnesota, Michigan State coach Duffy Daugherty suspended six players for curfew violations, five of whom were starters. The guilty team members did not suit up for Notre Dame, which was played and lost on the following Saturday, 24-12. Saddled with early season losses, injuries, and suspensions, Michigan State limped into its contest with Indiana. The oddsmakers didn't see it that way. The Hoosiers were pegged as six-point underdogs in spite of their unblemished record compared to Michigan State's five games in the loss column. Much of the analysis was based on strength of schedule. Most of Michigan State's losses were to nationally ranked teams, including probable Rose Bowl participant Southern California. Against similar opponents, Michigan State had soundly beaten Michigan and Wisconsin, whereas the Indiana margins of victory were razor thin. Sportswriters asked Coach Pont whether his players were insulted over the lack of respect by the oddsmakers. He responded, "Insulted? Probably, but I'm still completely in the dark as to what they're going to do in any game."

IU was ranked sixth in both UPI and the AP polls. Just ahead of them at fifth was their last opponent of the regular season, in-state rival Purdue and a contest that might decide the Big Ten championship. Minnesota lingered in tenth position in the UPI poll.

Rose Bowl chances increased with each victory. Only Michigan State, Minnesota, and Purdue stood between Indiana and a perfect regular season. It would take only two victories in those three games to ensure a Rose Bowl berth, Indiana's first. Michigan State knew the territory. They had conquered the Pacific Coast Conference, the forerunner of the Pac-8, on January 1, 1954 and 1956. The Spartans were the preseason choice to win a third straight Big Ten conference championship. This was not supposed to be a big game. Notre Dame coach Ara Parseghian commented in the *Indianapolis Star*, "Football is filled with surprises. There has been no greater surprise in 1967 than Indiana, a team that won only one game in 1966." *Lansing State Journal* sportswriter Bob Hoerner called IU "the biggest surprise in college football since the forward pass."

Although still dangerous, the Spartans didn't have the super strength of the 1965 and 1966 teams. Four starters were drafted by the NFL among the first eight picks in 1967. Duffy Daugherty lamented that "our players are playing their hearts out but they are either inexperienced or lack the physical ability to do the things we are asking them to do. We lost some of the country's outstanding defensive players." He added, "We can't reach into the Red Cedar and pull out a couple of linebackers, some halfbacks, and big linemen." They did look formidable in their shutout against cross-state rival Michigan at Ann Arbor on October 14.

Besides the insult leveled by the bookmakers and a chance at the Rose Bowl, Indiana had additional incentives. A defeat of Michigan State would tie Indiana University's all-time winning streak of eight games set in the Big Ten championship year of 1945. The Old Brass Spittoon was also at stake. This trophy was introduced in 1950 by Michigan State class president Eugene

McDermott to provide motivation for Spartan players to defeat Indiana. It bears the following inscription:
THE OLD BRASS SPITTOON

INAUGURATED BY THE
STUDENTS OF MICHIGAN
STATE COLLEGE AND
INDIANA UNIVERSITY
NOVEMBER – 4 – 1950

McDermott's idea must have worked. The Old Brass Spittoon had been showcased in East Lansing for fifteen of seventeen years. Some of the IU players didn't know it existed. Pont wanted it back.

Senior Kaz smelled the blood of the wounded Spartans. He had played against essentially the same Michigan State offensive line for three years. In the backfield, Dwight Lee was the leading rusher at 4.2 yards per carry. The fleet Hawaiian runner Bob Apisa averaged 4.1 and quarterback Jimmy Raye was solid and steady. There was no love lost on either side of the line of scrimmage.

Even though quarterback Frank Stavroff completed 23 passes against Michigan State in 1966, the IU team was soundly beaten and soundly beaten up. Kaczmarek retained that memory all year long. The normally affable linebacker was as serious as a funeral dirge. Kaz and his crew wanted to inflict some pain that day, physical and mental.

No one was more excited for this game than linebacker Kevin Duffy, who suffered a season-ending injury and almost lost his life in combat with Michigan State in 1966. In the beginning of the third quarter of that game, Duffy ran at Raye with his hands up in the air to prevent the Michigan State quarterback from throwing. Just as Duffy made contact, Raye ducked and buried his helmet in Duffy's left side. Duffy dropped to the ground in a clump. Kaczmarek ran over and yelled, "Get up, get up." Duffy was stunned. On the next play, he managed to stand

Michigan State

but could not move. His fellow linebackers assisted him off the field, where Dr. Bomba was waiting for him. Duffy thought he had broken some ribs but Bomba said, "No, your ribs feel fine." Duffy played the rest of the game.

There was a party planned that night and a particular coed Duffy wanted to see. He resisted the urge to take muscle relaxants and go to sleep. In the early evening he experienced severe cramps in his stomach. One of his friends took him to the infirmary, where the nurse recognized that he was in shock and sent him to the Bloomington hospital in an ambulance. Emergency doctors operated at once and removed his ruptured spleen. The season was over for Kevin Duffy. Michigan State sent him a game ball signed by all the players. He appreciated it, but he itched to get back on the field and play them again. His coaches quietly agreed that would never happen. They should have known better. Duffy was released from the hospital after a second operation just before spring practice and was used sparingly, but by fall he was ready and played in every game.

Michigan State won the coin toss and opted to receive. On the first play of the game, Indiana shifted three or four times into different formations before they ran their final defense. Doug Crusan returned to the Indiana huddle and said, "Those guys, you ought to hear them. Raye was yelling at them saying 'What are they doing?' and they answered, 'We haven't got a clue what they're doing.'" On the second play Michigan State was caught committing a personal foul. Three plays later Kaczmarek was penalized for grabbing Raye by his facemask. The discussions in the defensive huddle were intense. Kaz said a few times, "We are going to kill these motherf***rs!" Cordell Gill came up to Kaz later in the game and said in jest, "I cannot believe you graduated from a Catholic school." It was personal.

Still in the first period, on fourth and three on the IU 12-yard line, Michigan State opted to run rather than kick a field goal. The IU defense held thanks to a Crusan tackle. Later in the period Gonso threw an interception, and on the Gonso tackle out of bounds, IU was penalized for a personal foul. The

Cinderella Ball

penalty-ridden first period, marked by rough play, ended in no score.

Early in the second quarter Gonso lost the ball on a wild pitch out attempt at his own six-yard line, giving Michigan State the ball with first and goal. Kaczmarek called three different blitzes and after the third down Michigan State was still on the six-yard line. Offensive linemen looked at Raye and said, "We know they're coming but we don't know where." The Spartans settled for a field goal. Michigan State led 3-0.

It was a war and the referees could not keep up. Defensive end Bill Wolfe, from Decatur, Illinois, was a casualty. The 6'2", 215-pound Wolfe suffered a severely sprained ankle from a Michigan State helmet and had to be assisted off the field, and his quickness and agility were lost to IU for the rest of the game. Midway through the second quarter, Isenbarger was gang tackled and kicked in the head, knocking him out. The referees either missed or overlooked the infraction. When he awoke, he had to be carried to the bench, where he sat for the rest of the half and most of the third quarter trying to make the stars go away. Krivoshia, in for Isenbarger, kept the Spartans on their heels, pumping like pistons through the line with 11 carries for 53 yards. Isenbarger returned to the game for one series in the third quarter, but had to again be assisted off the field. Gonso finally got his offense rolling, hitting a 20-yard pass to Stolberg and a 16-yard pass to Al Gage. Gonso snuck in the end zone for the score to end the drive, which was aided by another Michigan State personal foul. Kornowa kicked the extra point, giving the Hoosiers a 7-3 lead.

Later in the quarter Doug Crusan returned to the huddle with a wide smile. Every time IU tackled Michigan star running back Bob Apisa, Duffy bent over him and said, "Get up you f***ing pineapple." Duffy laughed. "I called him a f***ing pineapple, and he's very upset and complained to the referee."

The referee barged into the IU defensive huddle and said, "Slow it down a little on this guy."

Duffy turned to him and replied, "We're trying to call the

defense and we don't have time for you to give us a lecture about how to talk to people on the other team." When the referee wouldn't leave, the players closed ranks, leaving the referee outside looking in.

In the third quarter the rain turned to snow, and a Michigan State punt was fumbled by Nate Cunningham and recovered by Jade Butcher on the Indiana eight-yard line. After a gain of two, Gonso was tackled at the line of scrimmage and pushed back into his own end zone for a safety. Gonso argued that he was stopped at the line of scrimmage and did not voluntarily step across the goal line into his end zone. Gonso was correct but the referee was not swayed. Perhaps he was disgruntled by the poor reception he received from Duffy and the Indiana defense. The Hoosier lead was cut to 7-5. Because of the safety, Indiana was required to kick to Michigan State from its own 20-yard line, which gave Michigan State favorable field position. The Spartans quickly took advantage and with the aid of a personal foul penalty against Indiana after the kick, scored a touchdown. A fake extra point kick netted them two points and a 13-7 lead.

After a possession exchange, Butcher called for a fair catch and was fouled. Gonso wasted the favorable field position with his second interception of the day, bringing the third quarter to a close. Michigan State 13, Indiana 7.

Early in the fourth quarter Gonso threw yet another interception. When IU got the ball back there was 6:33 left in the game, plenty of time for a rally. Pont wasn't troubled. He told Gonso, "Just go ahead with our basic football. Take your time, there's no hurry."

Gonso smiled and replied, "Don't worry, Coach."

Isenbarger looked up from the bench and signaled to Pont, "I'm ready." Sporting a big knot on his head, Isenbarger put the team on his shoulders. He gained 13, 14, and 12 yards and caught a pass from Gonso for another 15 yards. Terry Cole, quietly suffering from the flu, drove to the Michigan nine-yard line in three tries. Isenbarger scored the tying touchdown when he beat the defense around the right end, a one-yard run with 2:50 left to play. According to Joe Hamelin, *Indianapolis Star* sportswriter, Isenbarger accounted for 59 of the 69 yards in IU's last drive. The score was tied 13-13. Kornowa, who had not attempted an extra point since injuring his leg against Illinois more than a month before, came in for the kick. It was successful.

Michigan State had one more chance at victory, but their desperation pass was picked off by Kaczmarek, who was run out of bounds. About three yards off the field MSU running back Rich Berlinski struck Kaczmarek in the groin with his helmet. Kaz turned to Coach Plank and said, "Ernie, that SOB tried to really hurt me." A fracas ensued on the sideline and personal fouls were called on both teams. The game was over, but the teams were still fighting. IU ran out the clock for the win.

The victory over Michigan State marked the fifth late-game, come-from-behind effort of the season. In this contest they had to do it twice. Six of the eight margins of victory were 1, 2, 3, 4, 5, and 7 points. A jubilant Nate Cunningham expounded, "The margin of victory is not the important thing. We win the close ones. Isn't that the mark of a good team?

Duffy Daugherty commented after the game, "They scramble, hustle and never give up." *Lansing State Journal* reporter Bob Hoerner attributed the IU victory to hustle. He opined, "That's something you cannot measure by previous scores or by looking at films of games and you have to have it to win." Max Stultz of the *Indianapolis Star*, noting that throughout the game Isenbarger's kicks were unremarkable, wrote, "Isenbarger apparently has whipped an overpowering desire to run with the ball from punt formation."

Pont, after reminding the press that Mike Krivoshia went from a possible preseason All-American to backup status behind John Isenbarger, said, "There is no question that Mike played his finest game at Indiana University." Krivoshia ran 23 times for 92 yards. Pont awarded him a game ball.

Kevin Duffy reviewed the stats on the plane ride home.

Michigan State was able to gain only 176 yards, 122 on the ground and 54 passing. They essentially scored no points on the defense. They scored on a safety, a cheap field goal, and a cheap touchdown in the third quarter, and all because of offensive blunders. The victory and the play of the defensive unit closed an important loop for Duffy.

Pont turned forty on Monday following the game and was presented five cakes from players, the student athletic board, the athletic department, the downtown quarterback club, and an admirer. One of them had a rose placed in the middle with the words, "Happy Birthday, Happy New Year's." Another said, "Happy Birthday, John Our Coach of the Year." More than fifty people gathered for the cake presentation from the athletic department. With a mouthful of birthday cake, Pont called the 14-13 victory the team's best game of the year. He swallowed and said, "The team just never got rattled. Gonso called every play in our winning touchdown drive. If there's a better quarterback in the country at calling plays, let me see him." During the next few days there was a media frenzy. Pont spent most of his time on the telephone talking to people around the United States, including ABC and NBC. In answer to questions regarding IU's Rose Bowl chances and probable regular season finish, Pont was noncommittal. He said, "Boy you get rid of one thing and right away there's another one staring you right in the face. And this time it's Minnesota."

Ironically, optimism ran high except to a reticent Pont. A student, Sam Strois, penned a poem to the *Daily Herald Telephone*:

> For those who cannot figure
> Why our victory string has grown,
> The explanation's simple, folks,
> We're in the Twilight Zone.
>
> We'll beat the Gophers, that is true,
> And then we'll clobber ol' Purdue.

The Bloomington City Council expressed its support with a resolution that read:

> WHEREAS, this great team has won only 8 of the
> 10 games scheduled for the season, and
>
> WHEREAS, it is necessary to win one more game to
> assure a long-awaited Rose Bowl bid, and
>
> WHEREAS, we are certain of victory over Purdue,
> but desire an added cushion of one victory, now
>
> THEREFORE, be it resolved that the fervent and
> deep-felt prayers and best wishes of this Council
> and this City be conveyed to Coach Pont and his
> team, along with assurances that all good citizens
> are behind them in their arduous encounter with
> Minnesota this Saturday.

Pont wondered whether the physical beating in East Lansing would take a toll on the team. He thought about the local motel marquee that flashed the recommendation: "Make Your Pasadena Reservations Now" and said to himself, "It may be premature."

CHAPTER 12

MINNESOTA

Pont and company arranged to fly to Minneapolis on November 17, the eve of their showdown with the University of Minnesota. Pont was relieved to get away for the weekend and divert his attention from media and fan frenzy and back to the game he loved. When the Hoosiers reached Weir Cook Airport in Indianapolis, Marion County sheriff's deputies served a court order on the bewildered coach. It read, "Coach John Pont is hereby ordered to win the game against Minnesota." He was also charged with larceny for stealing eight games. Pont pled guilty and confessed to the officers that he would sure like to steal a few more.

A win over Minnesota would guarantee them a golden ticket: an invitation to the Rose Bowl, "the granddaddy of them all," the oldest college football bowl game. In 1946, the forerunners of the Pac-8 and the Big Ten entered into an agreement where the champion from each conference would play the other in the Rose Bowl on New Year's Day. The venue sold out every year since 1947 and inspired many other bowl contests, including the Sugar Bowl, Sun Bowl, and Orange Bowl. A loss to

Minnesota meant IU would probably not be going to any bowl games. Only conference champions were bowl-eligible.

Both camps were excited to put the Rose Bowl debate to bed. It was either going to be Minnesota or Indiana in Pasadena, not Purdue. Purdue was formidable with its league-leading 452.4 yards per game, but they were Rose Bowl ineligible because the Boilermakers had participated in 1966. The previous week, Purdue had clobbered Minnesota 41-12. Indiana did not need to clobber Minnesota. They just needed to beat them. In fact, all Indiana really needed to do was tie. Purdue's Leroy Keyes, referred to as the "Amazing Mr. Everything," and quarterback Mike Phipps, who had made fans forget "so last year" Bob Griese, looked forward to taking the field in a home game against Michigan State University with a share of the Big Ten title at stake. But the Rose Bowl invitation was just between Indiana and Minnesota; Purdue need not apply. Minnesota officials expected only 47,500 fans (capacity 63,430) to be on hand to root for their team. Many were a bit downhearted after enduring the defeat at Purdue and were reluctant to sit through a frigid day of football with their faith in their team shaken.

Rose Bowl fever was rampant in Bloomington. Ticket requests for the Rose Bowl were pouring in from all over the country, including California. Orwig said, "I'm receiving many letters from California and a lot of them are people we've never heard of." Orwig explained that he was unable to fill requests until priorities were established and until Indiana University earned the right to represent the Big Ten, which he hoped would be Saturday afternoon. The explanation did not curtail the requests.

Before Pont departed, he told the *Indianapolis Star* after a light physical workout that his unbeaten football team was prepared. He added that all his regulars were at full working speed and that included Gonso's shoulder injury and Isenbarger's head injury. Pont neglected to mention that right tackle Bob Kirk had been sick all week with the flu and didn't practice. Team physician Brad Bomba was concerned and so was Kirk, who called his parents and was directed to a local physician, who shot him up with penicillin. Kirk lost five pounds during the week. He wondered whether he could block. The Minnesota chill, close to freezing with 21 mile-per-hour winds, was brutal for Kirk. He played the game in his weakened state. Perhaps that was one reason Gonso was harassed in his backfield all afternoon.

A Minnesota chill was not the exclusive purview of Mother Nature. That summer, a few months before the game, racial tension erupted in Minneapolis with three nights of arson, assaults, and vandalism. The rioting was finally quelled by six hundred National Guardsmen, who, with the local police force wearing riot helmets and wielding shotguns, maintained an uneasy peace. Local press cited alienation and racism. Minnesota had a small black segregated population, a perfect cauldron for racism to flourish. Pont was the object of threatening calls, for example, "If you put your darkies on the field they and the rest of the team will suffer season-ending injuries after the game." Pont also neglected to mention that to the press nor did he share it with his players.

The midweek rankings placed the Hoosiers at fifth in both the AP and UPI surveys. IU even received one first place ballot in each poll. The *Manitowoc Herald-Times* established IU as a three-point favorite to beat Minnesota and go to the Rose Bowl. Local bookies took bets on Minnesota as a one-touchdown favorite. John Bansch opined in the *Indianapolis Star*, "Big, beautiful roses are waiting to be plucked off the icy plains of Minnesota today by Indiana's incredible football team." According to Associated Press sportswriter Charles Chamberlain, the game at Minnesota was a must for Indiana because it would be impossible to have to pin its Rose Bowl hopes on beating Purdue.

Minnesota would be the beefiest team the Hoosiers faced all season. The offensive line averaged 238 pounds and overall Minnesota averaged 204 pounds, outweighing Indiana by twenty pounds per man. During warmups, Snowden looked down the field at the Golden Gophers and whispered to Cunningham, "That's the biggest college football team I have ever seen in my life." Pont told his players in the locker room, "Our quickness will prevail against their size and strength." Warren Ariail instructed the players to don their helmets before taking the field. The locker rooms were located in the back of the end zone bleachers. They were open, and fans could drop items on people below. As the team ran this gauntlet, a few empty pint whiskey bottles came crashing down.

Coach (Gooner) Brown did not accompany the team to Minnesota. In anticipation of the Rose Bowl opportunity, Pont sent him to Los Angeles to scout the Southern California–UCLA game, the winner of which would probably be the Rose Bowl opponent.

Minnesota won the coin toss and elected to kick. Indiana ran off eight plays all the way to the Minnesota 35-yard line but, faced with a fourth-and-eight, opted to punt. Isenbarger's kick rolled dead on the Minnesota five-yard line. Minnesota ran ten plays as both teams played possession ball.

At the Indiana 34-yard line, a Minnesota pass was tipped by Bilunas and intercepted by Duffy. Bilunas, at 6'2", had also played basketball at Andrean High School in Gary, Indiana. He could leap. Gonso returned the favor with a fumble at the Indiana 40-yard line. As the quarter ended there was no score, but Minnesota was threatening at the Indiana six. The Gophers scored on the first play of the second quarter. The extra point was good, and Minnesota led 7-0.

On the ensuing possession Indiana could not make headway. Isenbarger kicked a 69-yard punt into the Minnesota end zone. After Minnesota punted the ball back on a three-and-out possession, Isenbarger, Butcher, and Gonso started to roll, to no avail. Gonso threw a pass to Butcher for a touchdown, but it was called back due to an ineligible receiver downfield. On fourth down Warner's field goal attempt from the 35-yard line was short.

Minnesota could do no better. The Gophers took over on

their own 20 and fumbled the ball away. It was recovered by tackle Jerry Grecco on the Indiana 49-yard line. Grecco, a six-foot junior, was a high school All-American from Andrean High School in Gary. His career was injury-plagued, but Pont counted on him for considerable playing time. Gonso was unable to move the ball, and Isenbarger again had to punt. On the runback, Minnesota committed its second personal foul of the day. Still in the game, the Indiana defense, led by Kaczmarek, Sniadecki, and Crusan, stopped Minnesota at their own 32-yard line. Gonso had time left in the first half and he gave it a good effort, running for four, three, and nine yards. He benefited from another personal foul against Minnesota, but he was unable to score. The rest of the first half was not eventful but for the fact that Minnesota committed its third personal foul on the next-to-last play.

Isenbarger took the second-half kickoff at his own 16-yard line and ran it back to the 24-yard line. The team began to jell as Gonso, Butcher, and Isenbarger put together a series of strong runs, and Gonso completed passes to Gage and Butcher. Gonso completed the touchdown drive with a one-yard run, and Kornowa's kick tied the score at 7-7. Minnesota returned the kickoff to the 32-yard line and after a long drive scored a touchdown. The extra point attempt was blocked by Sniadecki. The third quarter ended with the score Minnesota 13, Indiana 7.

The fourth quarter began with Minnesota incurring its fourth personal foul. According to *Star* reporter Max Stultz, "Gonso was getting smeared hard and often." Although the referees did their best and called a number of personal fouls, they missed most of them. On a pass attempt that went incomplete, Minnesota defensive tackle Ron Kamzelski put his hulking 240 pounds on Gonso and did not get up. Things weren't going well for Gonso anyway, and he was frustrated over the brutal treatment he was receiving at the hands of the Minnesota defense, particularly Kamzelski. With the defender laying on top of him, face to face, Gonso closed his fingers over the grill of Kamzelski's face mask and held tight while he slugged him in the midsection, then quickly placed his arms to his sides to protect his ribs, all out of the sight of the referees. Kamzelski couldn't move because of the death grip Gonso put on his face mask. He tried to return the punch but could not get up so he just pounded Gonso with left and rights to his sides. The referee, however, saw him flailing at Gonso and called a flagrant personal foul that sent Kamzelski to the showers. Gonso staggered to his feet with his teeth clenched. The referee turned to Gonso and said, "I know you had something to do with that." Gonso deadpanned, "It was a late hit and he just started beating on me." The personal foul put Indiana on the Gopher 42-yard line, but the drive stalled as Gonso tried for nine yards on fourth down and only made five.

To the thousands who had seen the Hoosiers beat the chart Saturday after Saturday in racing to eight straight victories, the scene had been set. It was time for Indiana's fourth-quarter heroics. One touchdown plus one extra point would make it 14-13. But not this time; if this game were a fairy tale, the witch would have eaten Hansel and Gretel.

According to the *St. Cloud Times*, "The last quarter magic which has helped the Hoosiers to a season of cliffhanger victories was gone Saturday. Instead, Indiana helped Minnesota to the end zone with some grievous bobbles." Minnesota scored on its next possession, and the extra point was again blocked by Sniadecki. A rare miscue by Jade Butcher on the kickoff gave Minnesota possession at the Indiana 23, which was converted immediately for a touchdown. As the game slipped away in the fourth quarter, Pont, undaunted, paced the sidelines like a father at 2:00 a.m. waiting for his daughter to come home. He shouted to everyone he could, "I want you to make up your minds right now: beat Purdue next week." Late in the game Gonso committed his second fumble, leaving Minnesota an easy score from the Indiana 33. The fourth-quarter outburst mercifully ended with Minnesota winning 33-7.

The game belonged to Minnesota. The Gophers carried

the ball 67 times and gained 326 yards rushing, with halfback John Wintermute going 135 yards in 23 carries. Minnesota quarterback Carl Wilson scored four touchdowns, passed for one, and rushed for 118 yards. Right guard Dick Enderly and tackle John Williams gave Doug Crusan a very tough day at the office.

At the end of the game the Minnesota fans flooded the field as the band played "California Here I Come." The *St. Cloud Times* recapped, "Minnesota football Gophers were flying high after beating Indiana 33-7 and are shaping up as the Big Ten's most likely candidate for the Rose Bowl. Minnesota must still beat Wisconsin but that should not be difficult at all. Indiana has to take on unbeaten Purdue. That gives Minnesota the edge for the postseason roses."

Bob Collins lost faith. He wrote in the *Indianapolis Star*, "The Hoosiers, who had shown nothing but poise in eight straight victories, could not find themselves—or opposing ball carriers." He went on to say that in what seemed like a heartbeat, a flick of an eyelash, Indiana was all the way out of it. Fellow reporter Max Stultz said, "The Hoosiers absorbed a fearsome 33-7 shellacking in what most likely was a showdown battle for the Rose Bowl berth."

In the locker room Pont called his team together. In a voice trembling with anger he said, "We just got it kicked out of us but this season is not over. Remember nobody gave us a chance before it started. This game is done but I'm damned if Purdue is going to beat us. Make up your minds that this is done. You've got two hours on a plane to think about it, then forget it. I'm going to look you right in the eyes and if you don't want to play next week, you won't dress. By golly we'll get ready. We'll get ready. We'll practice and we'll get ready. Maybe this is the way it was meant to be. How do you want to go out? Bob (Russell), Harold (Mauro), and Kenny (Kaczmarek) and the rest of you seniors just remember it was 51-6 (Purdue) last year. Think about it."

Gonso thought about it. He had lost two fumbles. In

Cinderella Ball

addition, he had committed a number of uncharacteristic errors including a pass to Gary Cassells, an ineligible receiver, and an attempted pass to Al Gage after crossing the line of scrimmage. His rushing yardage netted only 36 yards. He only completed four passes the entire game. Gonso didn't need two hours on the plane to think about it. He was ready to forget the Minnesota game immediately. Jade Butcher was also ready to forget the game and that uncharacteristic error he committed on a Minnesota kickoff.

In the Gopher locker room coach Murray Warmath was triumphant. He told reporters that they had a great week of practice and the boys wanted this game. He praised "a fine IU ball club that played a competitive game that was not reflected in the final score." He added, "My players hit their emotional peak for Indiana."

That night more than eight thousand fans met the team in the old basketball fieldhouse to welcome them back from Minneapolis. Pont was speechless and had to be coaxed to give a brief pep talk that confirmed he was already looking ahead to the Boilermakers the following week. He said to the adoring IU family, "Tonight, I think we just beat Purdue."

The next day, according to schedule, the team assembled at the Student Union to watch films. The coaches brought champagne and said, "Oops, we thought you guys were Big Ten champions." The teammates enjoyed the razzing and a glass of champagne while reliving their stunning defeat at the hands of the Gophers.

On Monday, Pont assembled the seniors before practice. He said to Doug Crusan and Gary Cassells, "You guys want to play in the Senior Bowl?"

They replied, "Of course."

Pont said, "Well then, you're going to play there because they've asked us for two players." He then turned to Kaczmarek and offered him the Hula Bowl in Hawaii, which Kaz readily accepted.

Pont took out of his pocket a *Star* article summarizing the

Minneapolis debacle and carefully read, "Indiana's eight game winning streak, most of its Rose Bowl aspirations and all of its share of the Big Ten Conference lead died here yesterday of self-inflicted wounds." He tacked it on the locker room wall, turned to all who were within earshot, and said, "We'll see."

CHAPTER 13
PURDUE

Purdue met Indiana at Memorial Stadium in Bloomington on November 25, 1967, to wrestle for the Old Oaken Bucket for the forty-third time. Nobody cared. Normally, possession of that old bucket stamped a seal of approval on the football campaign regardless of the team's record. A victory over its intense intrastate rival was a badge of glory worn by IU players and coaches all summer long. At one point, the IU-Purdue rivalry was so hot that the games were discontinued for two years. It took a decree from the governor to restart the series. There was much more in the balance on that day in 1967.

The Old Oaken Bucket is a traveling trophy that was first awarded in 1925. Indiana alumnus Dr. Clarence Jones and Purdue alumnus Russell Gray were appointed to find a suitable trophy. They came up with the Old Oaken Bucket and the concept of adding bronze P's and I's to a chain that would represent victories throughout the years. A bucket was found in a well on an Indiana farm and the rivalry had its tangible evidence of victory.

The Old Oaken Bucket refers to a poem written by Samuel Woodworth which began:

How dear to this heart are the scenes of my childhood,
When fond recollection presents them to view!
The orchard, the meadow, the deep-tangled wildwood,
And every loved spot which my infancy knew... !

And e'en the rude bucket that hung in the well —
The old oaken bucket, the iron-bound bucket,
The moss-covered bucket which hung in the well.

The verses were recorded by crooner Bing Crosby on June 14, 1941. The old 78 record did not outsell Crosby's "White Christmas," but it did expand the reach and knowledge of this symbol of one of the nation's greatest annual football battles.

Oaken bucket lore was hardly relevant in 1967 as the stakes spiraled higher. Purdue intended to claim its first undisputed Big Ten title since 1929, and for IU, victory meant a tie for the Big Ten championship, a trip to Pasadena and a history-making 9-1 season. It would also be the first victory in Bloomington over Purdue since 1947. There was an unlikely possibility. If Wisconsin beat Minnesota, Indiana would be invited to the Rose Bowl regardless of the outcome of the IU-Purdue game. An *Indianapolis Star* article on game day borrowed a catch phrase from an Ivory soap commercial and declared "99.44 percent of the world's population would agree that Minnesota will devastate Wisconsin." An even more unlikely scenario had both Indiana and Minnesota losing combined with an Ohio State win over Michigan. That would produce a three-way tie at 5-2 among the eligible teams. Under that scenario, IU would probably get the nod. They had waited too long. Ohio State was a seven-point underdog. Collins said, "The teams are playing for the whole deck. Never since the first undergraduates waxed their mustaches, skinned a pig and tried a new game called 'football' have Indiana and Purdue marched into battle against each other with such glittering sugar plums dangling before their eyes." He summed up, "The rope is stretched out tight and today it will snap and turn into a noose for Indiana or Purdue."

On the last weekend of September, when Indiana played its first game of the season against Kentucky, the world took little notice. For the last game of the regular season, more than 350 writers, photographers, and broadcasters were expected in Memorial Stadium. In addition, the contest was scheduled to be beamed around the world via the Armed Forces Network and broadcast live in Europe, North Africa, Iceland, and Greenland. It would be taped in the Pacific and played later when it was daytime in that part of the world. It was estimated that the game would have the broadest press coverage of any athletic event ever held in Bloomington. Orwig warned fans to start early to avoid a massive traffic jam. Not enough of the overflow crowd heeded his advice. Survivors were rewarded for their patience with "Pasadena A-Go-Go" buttons. Fans wearing black and gold, and there were plenty of those, did not accept the buttons. West Lafayette was less than a two-hour drive from Memorial Stadium. Purdue alumni, fans, and friends also trekked from throughout the Midwest to see one of the strongest teams in Boilermaker history.

Indiana was accorded little chance. Purdue was ranked third in the nation. Indiana had dropped to fourteenth after the shellacking they absorbed the prior week from Minnesota. Purdue had routed Minnesota 41-12 and had also beaten Notre Dame 28-21 when Notre Dame was ranked number one in the nation. A week earlier, Purdue vanquished Michigan State 21-7 to remain on top of the Big Ten with an unblemished record.

Purdue coach Jack Mollenkopf, affectionately referred to as "the Ripper," claimed he was bringing to Bloomington the best team he had coached at Purdue in his twenty years at the helm. Boilermaker halfback Leroy Keyes was legendary. This extraordinary football athlete played both ways in an era in which that rarely occurred. He was the leading rusher in the Big Ten, averaging 6.9 yards per carry, and was the nation's leading scorer. Many felt that because of his diversity Keyes was a better all-around football player than Southern Cal's O. J. Simpson. Directing traffic was Mike Phipps, who many thought was going to be a quarterback under construction. One reason he ably filled the cleats of the previous year's hero, Bob Griese, was because he had underrated but talented receivers. In addition, the Purdue defense was the stingiest in the Big Ten. The Boilermaker juggernaut was a two-touchdown favorite.

The underdog was ready. Pont knew he had a chance against Purdue, but he needed to make his team believe it. He practiced them vigorously all week. On Thursday, Thanksgiving Day, half of the team went to Dr. Bomba's house for dinner and the other half went to Pont's home for turkey and pep talks. He reiterated to his team what he had emphasized at a press conference earlier in the week. IU had won eight and three-quarters games and lost to Minnesota mainly because the team had failed to execute, particularly in the fourth quarter. He added that it was a lack of mental and physical alertness that beat them at Minnesota and they were not going to let that happen against Purdue. By Friday the team was convinced—with reservations.

Friday night after dinner at McCormick's Creek the team met with their respective coaches to finalize game plans. Defensive secondary coach Nick Mourouzis and linebacker coach Ernie Plank reviewed the Purdue offensive personnel and went over the plan for containing Leroy Keyes. Coach Plank motioned with his pipe while reminding his backfield corps that they could not just direct attention on Keyes. They had to respect the ability of fullback Perry Williams. Plank was prophetic.

The normally unflappable Harry Gonso was convinced but expressed a concern to offensive coach Bob Baker and center and guard coach Herb Fairfield. Fairfield played tackle for Pont at Miami of Ohio before entering the coaching ranks and had earned the trust of seniors Russell and Cassells and their colleagues on the offensive line. Gonso sought assurances. His battery mate, center Harold ("Monk") Mauro, who had started and played in every game, tore his gluteus maximus at

Minnesota and was not listed in the starting lineup. Stolberg was also a bit disconcerted. He, like many of the sophomores, was a bit high-strung. Stolberg always lined up on the opposite side of the huddle as Monk and while the play was called drank in his calming influence. Steve Applegate, a sophomore from Cincinnati who had been a freshman walk-on the previous year, was slated to start in Mauro's place. He was nicknamed "Plug" because at 5'10", 225 pounds he was built like a fireplug. Plug was strong and quick and got off the ball well. He had logged minutes in most games, but as a sophomore he lacked the seasoning of Mauro, a fifth-year senior. Applegate was a bit nervous as well. In his first starting role, he had to face a Purdue defense boasting all–Big Ten middle guard Chuck Kyle and 6'5", 260-pound Lance Olssen, a defensive tackle. Both were All-American nominees. Teammates Gary Cassells and Bob Russell, considered two of the best offensive guards in the Big Ten, assured Plug that they would assist.

Pont devised a simple game plan. He eliminated half of the offensive formations. He knew that the Purdue defense would key on the Gonso, Isenbarger, and Butcher option plays, so he devised his plan around the fleet fullback, Terry Cole, right up the middle. They practiced "Cole up the middle" all week.

Terry Cole was as nervous as a condemned prisoner eating his last meal. That night in the privacy of their room at the Canyon Inn just before going to bed, he confided to Jade Butcher, "You know, I've gotta have a good game. I want to get drafted and I haven't had a real good season."

Butcher said, "Geez, Terry, you've had a great season, man, you've done good."

Cole responded, "I've just got to do well and get in this draft after I graduate and get out of school."

Butcher said, "Well, it looks to me like, Terry, you're gonna have the best game of your career. I can just feel it."

The irrepressible Isenbarger was convinced beyond a doubt, beyond reason. Pont told Bob Hammel, sports editor of the *Bloomington Herald-Record*, that Isenbarger, before heading out of the locker room to meet Purdue, stepped in front of a full-length mirror with helmet in hand and said, "My name is John Isenbarger, sophomore halfback, Muncie, Indiana, 6'2", 193 pounds." When he noticed Pont, he said, "Just practicing for national television, Coach."

Local businesses were convinced. The week of the Minnesota game, a sign in a Bloomington restaurant said, "God is alive and playing defensive end for Indiana." After the Minnesota mishap the sign flashed a new message, "God was injured last week. He is expected back for the Purdue game."

Pundits did not agree. Michigan State coach Duffy Daugherty said, "Indiana shows what hustle, desire and effort can accomplish but Purdue is the only great team in the Big Ten." An article in the *St. Cloud Times* declared, "Although Indiana coach Johnny Pont is not 'throwing in the towel' it will take a near miracle to save the Rose Bowl trip for the Hoosiers following their 33-7 defeat at the hands of almost certain Rose Bowl-bound Minnesota."

After a week of drizzle and cold, the weather was clear and the temperature hovered in the high fifties, balmy for late November in southern Indiana, a delightful day for a football game. As IU took the field for pregame warmups, Gonso marveled to his teammates, "It's like God opened the skies." All of the more than fifty-five thousand seats were filled, including the three thousand temporary bleachers Orwig had set up in both end zones. The groundskeepers did their best to welcome the men from West Lafayette. They painted the turf a new shade of green and adorned the north end zone with Purdue colors, black and gold interlocking diamonds. The south end zone was all cream and crimson. The center of the field was adorned with a large red circle surrounding the letters "IU" in white. As fans entered the fieldhouse to the strains of "California Here I Come," they purchased roses from the vendors with tags that said, "We smell roses."

Purdue won the toss and elected to receive. They advanced the ball, but at the Indiana 49-yard line quarterback Mike

Phipps fumbled the ball to left tackle Doug Crusan. Gonso could not advance the ball, and Isenbarger dutifully kicked to the Purdue six-yard line. Purdue could do no better and punted the ball from deep in their own territory. As Indiana's second possession began on its own 49-yard line, Pont shared an observation with his quarterback. "Harry, we guessed right." The linebackers were spread wide to stop IU's array of sweep options. Gonso called the play: handoff to Cole up the middle. Cole, the only senior in the offensive backfield, ran 42 yards.

The IU confidence was palpable. The offense trash-talked the Purdue players without mercy, yelling in their faces. Isenbarger tried off tackle for two yards. Stolberg caught a pass from Gonso in the end zone that was nullified when the referee ruled he was out of bounds. Stolberg had one foot inbounds, which is all you need in college football. He argued the call to no avail. On third down Gonso found Butcher for a touchdown. Butcher was guarded by Keyes, Purdue's best weapon, but Gonso saw it as "just another case of one-on-one and Jade will beat that any time." Kornowa kicked the extra point. With 7:34 remaining in the first quarter it was 7-0 Indiana. Phipps retaliated on Purdue's next possession, sending Williams off right guard for the touchdown from the IU five-yard line. The score was soon 7-7. The quarter ended with no further scoring.

On the Boilermakers' first possession of the second quarter, Keyes lost a fumble that was recovered by Cal Snowden at the IU 37-yard line. Gonso drove the ball to the Purdue two-yard line, where Mike Krivoshia scored IU's second touchdown. Kornowa's kick went off to the right. It was 13-7 Indiana at 11:08 before halftime.

With less than two minutes before the end of the half, Gonso noticed that the Purdue center linebacker was deployed elsewhere. He gave the ball to Cole. Applegate executed a perfect block from his center position that sprang the speedy Cole, while Cassells drove his man away from the play. Cole flew through the hole. At the beginning of the play Butcher lined up wide to the right. On the snap he hurried to the middle to try to block the free safety out of the way before he could make a tackle. As Butcher approached the safety, Cole had already blown by both of them. Butcher never got to the safety, but there was no need. Cole was already gone, untouched for 63 yards and IU's third score. He fell in the end zone and Stolberg ran up to him, stuck his face into Cole's nose guard, and said, "T-Bear, you were so great." Cole looked up, smiled and replied, "I know." They both burst out laughing.

Caught up in the moment, Cole lofted the football into the end zone stands. After the game a lady contacted Cole saying she had the "touchdown football" and asked, "Would you sign it for her." Terry told her sure. When the lady brought the ball out to sign, Terry offered to purchase the ball. The lady told him no. She just wanted Terry to sign it. He did and the lady walked away with her prize.

The score was 19-7 after the Cole touchdown. Proper strategy would be to attempt a two-point conversion to bring the score back to parity with a three touchdown score: 21 points. The team had worked on the fake extra-point kick during practices. When that play is called, Butcher is to stay on the field. Pont called the fake but Butcher missed the signal and ran off the field. Harry took the snap from Applegate, briefly knelt down and fake held for the extra point, then bolted to his left to pass to Butcher. Butcher was not there. He was supposed to be in position to catch Gonso's pass but he was standing on the sideline right next to Pont. Pont turned to Butcher with his hands on his hips, looked at him, and said, "JADE!" That's all he said. Those piercing black eyes told the whole story. The official scorer called it a Gonso failure to complete a two-point conversion pass. The half ended with the score Indiana 19, Purdue 7.

In the third quarter, Isenbarger kicked a short punt. Leroy Keyes shouldered the team for two runs totaling 35 yards, and Phipps handed the ball to Williams for the touchdown. The extra point made it 19-14 in favor of Indiana. Purdue kept Indiana off the scoreboard for the rest of the third and all of the fourth quarter while desperately attempting to take the lead. Purdue held the ball for twenty plays, including a fourth down and two at the 50-yard line that Keyes converted. Midway through the rally Phipps went back to pass. Dave Kornowa drilled him right in the chest. Phipps's legs were still running but his back was on the ground.

Cole (48) on a romp.

Applegate (53) and Russell (64) spring Cole (48) for a touchdown run.

On the twentieth play, it was second down and goal at the IU four-yard line. All those sprint drills had paid off. The defense had stamina but was dispirited. In the defensive huddle, Brown Marks started a cheer. He said, "I got that feeling. It's time to hit. This team won't quit. We don't take no shit." The team joined the cheer as they got in their stances. When both lines hit, the IU defense did not budge. Purdue fullback Perry Williams headed for the end zone, and Kaczmarek hit him square in the chest. Stolberg stood next to Pont on the sidelines and watched as the ball popped out and bounced around through Kevin Duffy's legs and right out in the open. It seemed to Stolberg that the play was unwinding in slow motion. Hoosier safety Mike Baughman pounced on it. It was his first fumble recovery of the year.

The Hoosiers had to punt from deep within their own territory. Applegate had been hiking the ball with a broken wrist suffered before the end of the first half. He played through the pain. Disregarding his own injury, Monk went in for Plug and hiked the ball to Isenbarger, who kicked it over the head of the Purdue safety, 63 yards, his longest of the year. Keyes came in for one play and trotted back to the bench. He could not raise his hands above his shoulders. He had been hit three or four times in the ribs with helmets that had steel facemasks, all perfectly legal under the rules of the day. In spite of his absence, the Boilermakers moved the ball to midfield. On fourth down, as Phipps went back to pass, Cal Snowden tackled him for a loss of nine yards. IU took over on downs with 2:30 left in the game. With a minute to play and IU unable to move the ball, Isenbarger trotted over to the sidelines and asked Pont, "Shall I pass or kick the ball?" Pont implored his versatile athlete, "Kick the ball out of there, John. Just kick it out." Isenbarger kicked the ball into the Purdue end zone, giving the Boilermakers a final opportunity to win the day from their own 20-yard line. Phipps, earning his nomination as a potential All-American, passed Purdue all the way to the IU 22-yard line but that was as far as he could go. The game ended Indiana

19, Purdue 14. Tears were shed that day. Tears of joy and tears of disappointment and disbelief. That would be expected in a hard-fought match with so much at stake.

According to Jim Taylor of the *Toledo Blade*, "When the game ended it seemed as if the entire state exploded onto the field." He was not entirely correct. The part of the state representing Purdue sat stunned. The IU fans that chose not to storm the field stood and screamed and roared. The IU band again struck up "California Here I Come." Pont was lifted by Jim Sniadecki and Eric Stolberg and carried across the field. John McKesson of the *Indianapolis Star* observed, "It looked for a moment like Pont would break apart like a wishbone as his players seemed to go in two different directions before they all merrily fell to the turf." Fans leaving the stadium by the thousands bought out the rest of the roses on their way to celebrate. They grabbed the roses so fast that vendors couldn't keep track. They also bought every piece of memorabilia available, including IU buttons and sweaters.

Terry Cole, bolstered by the confidence of his roommate and best friend, rushed for 155 yards and one touchdown. He was named MVP of the game and Midwest Back of the Week. In the locker room he sobbed as he said, "I wanted this, my God, but I wanted this." He thanked Applegate for his clutch block. The defensive unit harassed Keyes and disrupted his rhythm. Keyes had dropped a sure touchdown pass at the Indiana five-yard line, lost another first-down pass in Indiana territory, and fumbled on a fourth-down play to end a Purdue rally. Kaczmarek had a game-high 15 tackles and caused the fumble that saved the game. He was named Midwest Lineman of the Week. On hearing of the honor, he responded, "This was the most important game of my life." Pont was named Midwest Coach of the Week. In a break with tradition the team elected to award a game ball to Coach Pont. The victory over Purdue brought the regular season to an end. Collins described it as a wild and wonderful march of Indiana's Happy Hooligans in two words: "In Credible."

In Pont's postgame remarks he said, "Last week we were playing for the Rose Bowl instead of Minnesota. This week Purdue was more important in our minds than anything else!" He paused, then added, "In all my years of coaching I don't think I've ever seen a finer offensive player than Leroy Keyes." Pont had not seen another 1967–68 Heisman candidate, Orenthal James (O. J.) Simpson, who, as those words were spoken, was engaged in vanquishing his team's archrival, UCLA. Running at halfback for the University of Southern California, he carried his team to a Rose Bowl invitation with an exhilarating 64-yard touchdown run in the fourth quarter that tied the game (the extra point provided the win).

In the Purdue locker room, the Ripper (Coach Mollenkopf) called the experience one of their most disappointing losses. And in the Minnesota locker room after the Gophers bested the Wisconsin Badgers in a surprisingly close game, coach Murray Warmath made the case for his team. He said, "If Indiana is chosen, we should file a protest. We handed IU its only defeat. We ripped Indiana decisively 33-7. We should be going to Pasadena." Purdue athletic director Red Mackey and Ripper Mollenkopf took a different tack. They praised the Hoosiers for their season and wished them well. In his sports column on Monday, Hammel of the *Daily Herald-Telephone* cited the fact that Indiana beat Purdue and Purdue tore Minnesota apart. He concluded the Hoosiers have every right to go to the Rose Bowl. John Carmichael of the *Chicago Daily News* summed it up: "Strike up the band for Indiana, the people's choice."

After the game, half the fans went to Nick's or Ye Olde Regulator. The rest seemed to be packed in the Orwig home—upstairs, downstairs, in the kitchen. The phone rang and after a moment Orwig put the receiver down. He shouted, "We're going."

Purdue

IU is Rose Bowl bound!

1967 Indiana Hoosiers Regular Season Schedule and Results

Date	School		Opponent	Conf		Pts	Opp
Sep 23, 1967	Indiana		Kentucky	SEC	W	12	10
Sep 30, 1967	Indiana		Kansas	Big 8	W	18	15
Oct 7, 1967	Indiana	@	Illinois	Big Ten	W	20	7
Oct 14, 1967	Indiana		Iowa	Big Ten	W	21	17
Oct 21, 1967	Indiana	@	Michigan	Big Ten	W	27	20
Oct 28, 1967	(10) Indiana	@	Arizona	WAC	W	42	7
Nov 4, 1967	(7) Indiana		Wisconsin	Big Ten	W	14	9
Nov 11, 1967	(6) Indiana	@	Michigan State	Big Ten	W	14	13
Nov 18, 1967	(5) Indiana	@	Minnesota	Big Ten	L	7	33
Nov 25, 1967	Indiana		(3) Purdue	Big Ten	W	19	14

CHAPTER 14

WE'RE GOING

Sunday morning, November 26, 1967, Bill Orwig awoke with the joy that he had entered the lore of Indiana University, perhaps not with the prestige of Nobel Prizes, Crest toothpaste, or the Kinsey Institute, but close. Lopsided losses to Purdue, sanctions and probations, and Phil Dickens would be mere footnotes to his legacy. Indiana had laid a foundation of what he knew would be a long tradition of winning football. Bill was awash in the warmth of congratulations, particularly from colleague and friend, President Elvis Stahr, who had promised his full support and personal presence in Pasadena.

Orwig was going to be busy in the month of December, tasked with a myriad of details including tickets, tour packages, accommodations for not only the team and its army of support but also the IU band and the all-important alumni—and floats. He hadn't thought about floats. Whose responsibility was that? The last time he worked the Rose Bowl he was an assistant coach for Michigan. He did know that the Rose Bowl event would be worth millions to Indiana University, football, floats, and all.

He mused, "January 1, 1968, a Rose Bowl date with the

University of Southern California—what could be better to celebrate my 61st birthday than with a victory? If IU wins Coach Pont promised me the game ball as a birthday gift." He rolled out of bed. Every day had to count.

After Mass on Sunday morning, John Pont retreated to his office to set the practice schedule for the team and to list what needed to be accomplished before departing for California. The NCAA limited the number of practices between the end of the regular season and New Year's Day. To allocate those valuable dates in the best interest of the team, Pont decreed that the Hoosiers would not formally practice until December 14, a hiatus of more than two weeks. During that time Pont hoped that the players would maintain fitness by running and working on their own in small group sessions. Captain Doug Crusan responded, "There's not a chance this team will get out of shape." He made sure the team continued its running drills even when barred from the outdoors by cold rain.

The next day, Pont listened to broadcaster Howard Cosell on his national radio show. Cosell joined with the rest of the nation when he said that John Pont must be chosen Coach of the Year. Before the Purdue game, Cosell had repeatedly referred to IU as a bunch of overachievers who did not deserve their top ten ranking. In response, Cosell received fifty telegrams from Indiana. One was from Jim Sniadecki on behalf of the football team. It simply said, "See you in Pasadena." He signed it, "Fighting Hoosiers." On this Monday, his first show after the game, he said, "Once they beat Purdue they were entitled to their rating."

The life of student senator Steve Tuchman, cochair of the IU Student Rose Bowl Committee, became more complicated and frenzied after the victory over Purdue. When he accepted the offer from student body president Guy Loftman to serve as secretary of student services the previous fall, roses were not on anyone's mind. Tuchman's sole duty was to organize the annual student trip to Europe for the summer of 1968, and go on it. He did attend a "just in case" Rose Bowl meeting earlier in the month, but the Minnesota loss dashed his hopes and returned his mind to studies of history and anthropology and applications to law schools. By Sunday morning, the euphoria he felt while leaving Memorial Stadium and walking back to his suite in Briscoe Quad had given way to a realization that it was his responsibility to administer the student trip packages to Pasadena.

Professor Frederick C. Ebbs, IU director of bands and leader of the IU Marching Hundred, didn't waste a moment on Sunday. He had a month to conceive and rehearse a halftime show that would be seen by more than a hundred thousand fans and fifty million more throughout the world. His material would be fresh, so his team would require more practice time than the football squad. Because the Indiana winter would limit marching practice, he needed to schedule "two-a-days" every day after arriving in California. In addition to the halftime show, the band had to prepare for the Rose Bowl Parade and a number of other gigs. Ebbs had joined the university faculty on September 1, the first day of football practice. He had no idea he would be "coaching" a Rose Bowl team. Unlike Pont, he had been there before. He conducted the Iowa Hawkeye Marching Band in performances in the Rose Bowl on January 1, 1957, and January 1, 1959.

That night 6,500 persons attended a victory rally in the fieldhouse. As the celebration began, Coach Pont was greeted with a standing ovation by fans who chanted, "We love Pont, We love Pont." He was given a set of silver goblets from the senior class and a rose lei from the student body. He was also presented the Old Brass Spittoon for his victory over Michigan State and the Old Oaken Bucket for his triumph over Purdue. Pont stated his intention to beat Southern California and said, "Actually my coaching staff is so good that all I have to do is drink coffee and tell John Isenbarger to punt." Herbert Smith, assistant dean of students, announced that IU had signed a contract with Studentaire of Chicago, a division of Alumni Holidays, Inc., for a five-day trip to California at a student cost of $240. The package included round-trip plane fare, hotel accommodations at a choice of four hotels, continental breakfast, reserve grandstand seats for the parade with a box lunch, a New Year's Eve party open only to students on the tour, and all ground transfers. Tickets to the game were not included. Next on the dais, former president Herman B. Wells claimed, "I've watched IU football for 47 years and there has been no finer day than Saturday." He confessed he had tears running down his cheeks as the game ended. The rally lasted past midnight.

Gary Cassells missed the entire affair. He left for New York right after the Purdue game to appear with Bob Hope on television as a member of the National Football Writers Association All-American team. Cassells spoke with the three University of Southern California players who made that team, O. J. Simpson, Ron Yary, and Adrian Young. He commented to his teammates upon his return to Bloomington, "Boy, is that Yary big (6'6", 270). I'm awfully glad to see him on the offensive team." Simpson struck Cassells as a sharp guy. In class the following week, all Cassells could do was daydream and doodle roses.

President Stahr also did not attend the rally. He published his explanation in the *Indiana Daily Student* the following Tuesday:

> Heartiest congratulations to the Big Red, coach Pont, and his staff. I deeply regret that a long-scheduled meeting of the Commission on Federal Relations of the American Council on Education required my presence in Washington Sunday night during the victory celebration. I am sure that the thousands upon thousands at the Field House conveyed the great sense of pride and admiration which thousands more throughout the state and nation share in your triumphant team effort. The spirited response of the student body is a

gratifying indication of the strong backing that your achievement has earned. You can count on all-out support in the Battle of the Roses.

Elvis J. Stahr
President

Orwig need not have worried about floats. Governor Roger D. Branigin had appointed former governor Harold W. Handley to chair the Indiana Rose Bowl Float Fund Committee. Handley called a meeting for Monday morning at the statehouse to finalize plans to raise twenty thousand dollars to provide an Indiana float in the Tournament of Roses Parade. Committee members included John V. Barnett, Eldon Campbell, Carl R. Dortch, and Robert B. McConnell. The committee called for contributions. There was enough wealth around Handley's table to build the Indiana float from spare change. It was oversubscribed. Handley explained that only two floats were allowed in the parade from a single state, one from the state itself and the other from the university. Stahr appointed a committee to create the Indiana University float, which would be a joint effort with the city of Bloomington. The previous year Indiana's Rose Bowl float won second place in competition among states and Purdue's float was judged best in the educational division.

The theme of the 1968 parade was "Wonderful World of Adventure." There was a requirement that every float in the Tournament of Roses parade be completely decorated with fresh flowers. The Indiana floats, like the great majority, were built by professional float builders on site in Pasadena to required specifications: forty feet long, twenty feet wide, and seventeen feet high. They tended to be low in the front and higher in the rear. The shaping was created usually with a one-inch mesh chicken wire that was stretched and then fastened over the entire float. It was sprayed with a polyvinyl material, which provided the surface for decorating. The insertion of the fresh flowers normally began approximately 48 hours before the parade with the heartier blossoms applied first. All kinds of flowers were used, including orchids, marigolds, snapdragons, and chrysanthemums. Some of the more delicate flowers were placed on the floats only a few hours before the parade began.

Throughout the city of Bloomington, the Rose Bowl invitation bound the university and the town together as never before. Signs supporting the team adorned nearly every business. Bloomington hosted the Indiana University football squad and staff at a Rose Bowl kickoff banquet on Sunday, December 17. The invocation at the event was delivered by Reverend Robert Kirk Sr., pastor of Bethel AME Church. Reverend Kirk was the father of Rose Bowl team member Bob Kirk. John Hooker, the mayor of Bloomington, presented each of the players with a gift (small to avoid a violation of NCAA rules) and each of the coaches with a television set. Warren Ariail was cited for his talent of healing and was handed a silver teapot. Walking off the stage he loudly grumbled, "What the hell am I supposed to do with this goddamn piss pot?" He wanted a TV.

Two days later on December 19, the team was feted at the fieldhouse by the Indiana University student body. More than three thousand cheering students honored the team. Pont ran away from the field in the annual voting for Coach of the Year, receiving more than 54 percent of the 770 votes cast by members of the National Football Writers Association. The turnout would have been higher except many students had left campus for their winter holiday. This would be the last public function for the Indiana players, who were scheduled to leave the next day. They had endured almost a week of practices in cold and rain in Indiana and were looking forward to drills in the California sun. Pont introduced his team to enthusiastic cheers. Bob Hammel of the *Daily Herald-Telephone* wrote, "The choice of Pont for coach of the year was like a Russian election, how could it have gone any other way?" During the introductions, no one was more euphoric than defensive back Dave Evans, president of the senior class. Evans was placed on the roster when sophomore tackle Tom DeMarco declined to make the trip. DeMarco was named to the squad to replace starting offensive right tackle Bob Kirk, who had been injured in practice and underwent emergency knee surgery at Bloomington Hospital that day. Al Schmidt was promoted to fill Kirk's position at right tackle. Defensive tackle Bill Wolfe also was injured in practice that week and was listed as questionable.

Collins presents Pont with Coach of the Year award.

Cinderella Ball

Bob Collins, sports editor of the *Indianapolis Star*, was the master of ceremonies. Collins said there had never been a team in football history like the 1967 Indiana crew. He recapped the Purdue victory and referred to the Rose Bowl as a little game they used to play out on the West Coast while Indiana fans sat at home waiting for the nets to go up on the basketball hoops. He said he was disappointed that Santa Claus was not present, but Purdue coach Jack Mollenkopf, known earlier in his career as "Fat Jack," declined his invitation. Collins asked, "Did you ever in your wildest LSD trip believe that Indiana had so much as a snowball's chance in the place where all sportswriters and football coaches go, to finish this season 9-1 and represent the Big Ten in the Rose Bowl? This team has staged more comebacks than a drunk trying to go up a down escalator." He added, "There is one national championship that has not been completed and won't be until after the bowl games. The Football Writers Association of America could theoretically pick IU if they beat Southern Cal."

President Stahr and Bill Orwig addressed the jubilant crowd. Orwig declared, "I am full of humility for the results the boys have brought to Indiana." President Stahr received an ovation when he said, "USC may be favored by fourteen but Indiana is favored by millions. I wouldn't trade this team for any other team. I wouldn't trade this coach for any two coaches in the nation. They are the best team in the country, both on and off the field."

He also repeated his comments to the team, which were prepublished in the *Daily Student* that day:

> To the BIG RED:
>
> Indiana University is proud of you. Together you have given the followers of I.U. football the most exciting season in memory and have revived a spirit here that is strong and fine.
>
> This season will be memorable not only for the records you wrote into football history but for the dramatic flourishes you gave each victory and the

never-say-die determination and belief in each other that have brought you so very far down victory road.

The personal discipline, the individual endeavor, and the physical tax which underlay your achievements on the field are all the more appreciated because they were merged into a magnificent TEAM effort, an effort we feel confident will bring an I.U. victory in the Rose Bowl.

We salute you, one and all, with gratitude and resounding congratulations.

The *Daily Student* also published a letter from Chancellor Wells:

I thank The *Daily Student* for the opportunity to say publicly what I already have said to Coach Pont and his staff and through Coach Pont to members of the Varsity football squad.

The University today stands in the reflected glory of a great football team. Wherever I have gone this fall I have found people talking about Indiana's team and talented coaching staff which have established such a remarkable and extraordinary record. It is not only the record but the manner in which it has been achieved that has caught and held the attention of the students, faculty, alumni, friends of the university, and the public.

To say that we are proud of the team and of Coach Pont and his colleagues is a faint expression of the feeling which I am sure is in the heart of each and every student in the University.

Tuchman reminded students to bring everything in their official tour trip packet, including boarding pass, valid ID, continental breakfast coupons, New Year's Eve coupon, and baggage tickets. He also warned students that the legal drinking age in California is twenty-one and that the Los Angeles police would be at each hotel where the students were staying to strictly enforce that law. He and his crew sold pennants, buttons, and bumper stickers to raise money for entertainment and souvenirs for students attending the Rose Bowl. Buttons read "Kiss me, I'm a Hoosier," "We Believe," and "O. J. Who?" The bumper stickers read, "Indiana U. Rose Bowl '68" and the pennants read, "Pasadena, Rose Bowl '68."

Harry Gonso, selected as the team's most valuable player by members of the squad, commented on Southern California and said, "Coach Pont told us they have four All-Americans. On January first we will have twenty-two All-Americans." He also said that "O. J. is a great back but we've got one to equal him in John Isenbarger."

The event closed with the singing of "California Here I Come" to new words:

> Pasadena here we come,
> Pump us up and watch us run.
> We played 'em, we slayed 'em, we're No. 1.
> We'll beat you, defeat you, just before the final gun.
> The Happy Hooligans having fun,
> Punt John, punt John, please don't run.
> Mind Coach Pont, that sonofagun,
> Pasadena, here we come.

Wednesday, December 27, began a mass movement of Hoosiers to Los Angeles. Seventeen hundred flew to the West Coast on chartered planes. The next day was the biggest traffic day in the history of the Indianapolis Airport according to Edwin G. Petra, director of the Airport Authority. Twenty-seven charter flights with an estimated four thousand persons left for California beginning at 5:00 a.m. More flights left over the next few days. Rough estimates of Hoosier fans were in the twenty thousand range. Los Angeles welcomed its tourists in the usual way, with dense fog. By Thursday the Los Angeles airport was closed to all inbound traffic, and planes were rerouted to Ontario, California, fifty miles away.

On USC's University Park campus two miles southwest of downtown Los Angeles, USC coach John McKay and his squad, representing the Pac-8, were preparing to meet the Hoosiers, smaller but quicker than any of the teams they played during the season. This would be USC's sixteenth appearance. Unlike the Big Ten, the Pac-8 had no rule against a team going to the Rose Bowl in consecutive years. McKay, who had coached teams in the Rose Bowl twice before, including a loss to Purdue in 1967, responded to Pont's quote, "I don't know what they are going to do next," with, "You can't scout a team when the other coach admits he doesn't know what to expect. How in the world am I supposed to know?" The bookmakers thought they knew. Las Vegas character Jimmy the Greek installed the University of Southern California as a 14½ point favorite. Purdue coach Jack Mollenkopf disagreed. "I think Indiana has an excellent chance. The Hoosiers have confidence and good speed." It would be the seventh time that season that IU went into a game as an underdog.

Indianapolis Star special writer Jeff Smulyan, a junior at the University of Southern California majoring in history and telecommunications, noted that the Trojans' hard-nosed defense provided much of the momentum for their 9-1 season. Led by All-Americans Adrian Young, a linebacker, and end Tim Rossovich, the Southern California defensive unit held opponents to 2.07 yards per carry. Only nine touchdowns were scored against the defensive team all season. Smulyan added that Young intercepted four passes against Notre Dame quarterback Terry Hanratty, and Rossovich batted down three more. Against UCLA the Trojan defense held Heisman Trophy winner Gary Beban to negative yards rushing. The Trojans' only loss came against Oregon State on a muddy field by a score of 3-0. Smulyan, an Indianapolis native, invited his family—including his father, mother, brother Jimmy, and sister Dale with her new husband Zeke Friedlander, all IU fans—to join him at the game. Smulyan rooted for USC.

Cocaptain Tim Rossovich was fearsome—and nuts. "Timbo"

didn't just tackle you. He wiped you out. Coach McKay described him with a smile. "A big boy, an intelligent boy, but above all, a mean boy." According to *Sports Illustrated*, "He jumped out the window of his girlfriend's sorority house one night. He wasn't supposed to be there and he heard the security guards were coming. He ran right through the room where sorority mother, Clemmie, was playing cards and dived head first out the window. The room was on the second floor. Clemmie didn't look up. She knew him pretty well." Rossovich said, "It was a bad week for me. I fell off two roofs and set fire to myself jumping over a car."

The offensive line was led by Outland Trophy winner Ron Yary (6'6"). A journeyman halfback could have a career game trotting through holes Yary created, and USC had O. J. Simpson, who led the offense. He was elusive and fast. Simpson, whose nickname was "The Juice," was named after his aunt's favorite French actor. His early life was challenging. His parents divorced when he was five, and as a child he developed rickets and wore braces on his legs. He was raised by his mother in housing projects in the Potrero Hill neighborhood, where he joined a street gang called "The Persian Warriors" at age thirteen and was briefly incarcerated at the San Francisco Youth Guidance Center. He found his calling at the City College of San Francisco, a member of the California Community College System, playing football as a running back and a defensive back. He was named to the Junior College All-American Team as a running back and earned an athletic scholarship to the University of Southern California. He led the nation in rushing in 1967.

After the Trojans reviewed the Minnesota-Indiana tape, McKay declared, "I'm glad it's Indiana. Simpson opined that he would rather play the bigger and slower Gophers than Indiana," but then he tossed off, "The Hoosiers are going to have to be very lucky."

We're Going

THE PAC-8

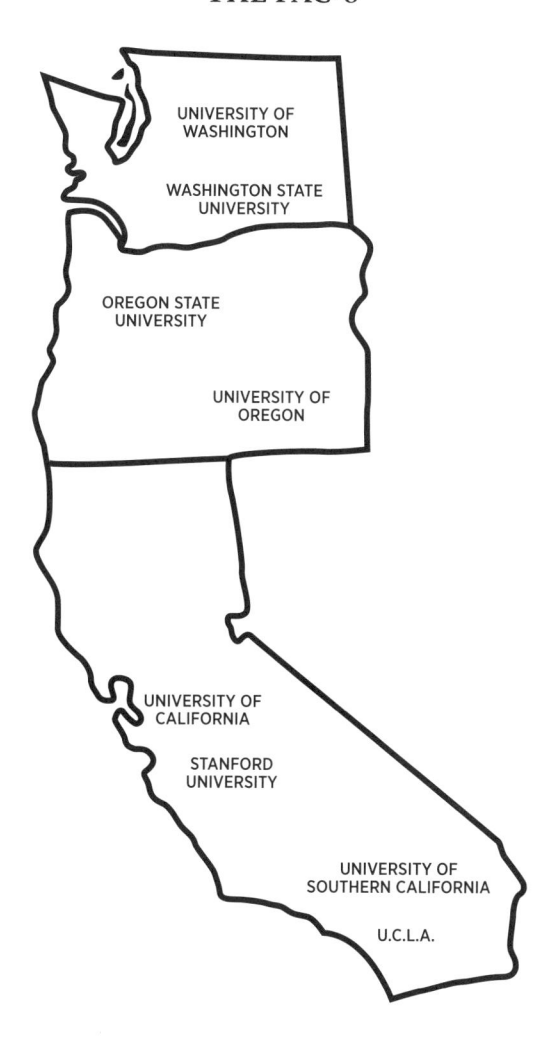

- UNIVERSITY OF WASHINGTON
- WASHINGTON STATE UNIVERSITY
- OREGON STATE UNIVERSITY
- UNIVERSITY OF OREGON
- UNIVERSITY OF CALIFORNIA
- STANFORD UNIVERSITY
- UNIVERSITY OF SOUTHERN CALIFORNIA
- U.C.L.A.

CHAPTER 15

THE ROSE BOWL

The Hoosiers arrived in Los Angeles on December 21 and were met by Rose Bowl representatives, including tournament president H. W. Bragg and Queen Linda Strother and her court. The team was transported by motorcade to the Huntington-Sheraton Hotel in Pasadena, where they held a press conference and a photo session. A reporter asked Pont how he sold players on going to Indiana. Pont replied, "I told them it would be a challenge and if they did the job, people would always remember them."

"How can you sell something so negative?" the man asked.

Pont quipped, "They sell life insurance every day."

While the team checked into their hotel, an anonymous donor gave Pont a glass slipper and wished his Cinderella team good luck at the ball.

That night the IU players enjoyed the famed "Beef Bowl," the annual eating competition between the two Rose Bowl teams at Lawry's Prime Rib in Beverly Hills. IU finished second in every category. They lost in mashed potatoes 60 pounds to 40 and were wiped out in creamed spinach 55 pounds to 32. The main bout wasn't close. IU consumed 289 pounds of beef to USC's

321. In the losing effort, Brown Marks claimed he ate fifteen cuts of prime rib. There were complaints that USC was allowed to field more players at the buffet.

Hoosier practices were held at Brookside Park, a semipro baseball park in the shadows of the Rose Bowl. Running continued to be a large element in Pont's training program. Kaz completed his running assignment with a slide into home plate. Curious crowds packed the stands to watch IU go through its paces. McKay closed his practices to the public.

Between workouts the team was treated and feted all over town. The players were furnished with Rose Bowl cars and chauffeurs. Pont imposed a curfew of 10:00 p.m. and assessed a 40-yard sprint for every minute they checked in late. The chauffeurs took them into Los Angeles to visit nightclubs and then tried to beat the clock. One night, Foster, Karl Pankratz's chauffeur, missed a turn and found himself heading the wrong way on the LA Expressway. Pankratz and his pals owed the coaches forty 40-yard dashes.

The day after the team arrived in California, they went to Disneyland, and the Southern Cal team was there too. Dressed in matching blazers and ties, they looked like giants compared to the Indiana guys. The USC team was standoffish. O. J. Simpson was the only player who walked over and interacted with the IU squad. During the afternoon, the people mover at Disneyland got stuck. John and Sandy Pont and many of the players had to wait for an emergency crew to offload them. On a later outing to Universal Studios, Pankratz took a picture with Frankenstein that appeared in the national papers.

The team attended two Christmas parties, a private affair on Christmas Eve at the Huntington-Sheraton and another on Christmas Day sponsored by the Tournament of Roses Committee. At the Christmas Eve party, each player was presented a watch engraved with his name and position on the back. On the face was "Indiana Football 1968" and "Rose Bowl." One watch was reserved for injured comrade Bob Kirk, on crutches recovering from knee surgery. At the party on

The Rose Bowl

Christmas Day, the players received binoculars and transistor radios.

On December 29, a banquet and program for more than two thousand guests was hosted by the Big Ten Club of Southern California at the Palladium. The Indiana University ticket office sent back 1,500 mail orders that could not be filled. The sellout affair featured the Smothers Brothers and Indiana University's Singing Hoosiers. Former governor Harold W. Handley was the emcee.

At the banquet Elvis Stahr said, "Our surprisingly Big Red team has confounded predictors and opponents all year and has almost defied diagnosis. If you've seen them play you will agree, something new has been added to that team. Just what that is, there are as many explanations as there are sportswriters. They have pride and they have desire and they love to play football."

The "Singing Hoosiers" could perform anything from Broadway musical hits to operatic selections. They entertained audiences from across the United States and around the world and were described as "one of the finest popular music groups in the U.S. today." In addition to the Palladium appearance, the schedule of performances for the Singing Hoosiers Rose Bowl tour included the Huntington Hotel for the National Exchange Club, the Pasadena Auditorium, the UCLA Basketball Classic, the Tournament of Roses Director's Dinner, and Disneyland. The repertoire for the entirety of the tour included thirty-nine songs, consisting mostly of a variety of Broadway musical numbers and music of Indiana composers, including Hoagy Carmichael and Cole Porter.

Hoagy Carmichael wrote a new song to be presented by him and the Singing Hoosiers at the Big Ten Banquet titled "To the Team."

> **To the Team**
> The big, tall maples on the Campus
> Lift their branches proudly to the sky,
> And while they're swayin' they keep saying'

Cinderella Ball

We'll be even taller bye 'n bye;
Their leaves a-rustlin' down below are
Whispering, Old I.U. is much the best,
A beech-nut tree with knarled knee is
Beating on his ivy-covered chest;
Now listen, boys, the beech is sayin'
They ain't nothin' yet that you can't do,
The East is East 'n West is West, but
Indiana's sumpin' special, too –
Us trees'll wait in snowy silence
As we've done for 80 years or more,
To Hear that youthful cry of vict'ry
Thunder from across the Campus floor.
So pack your gear – get out o' here
And see if you can pass the final test –
But a little hick'ry sapling said,
From an old Arbutus bed,
"Go out and conquer the West!"
The big, tall maples on the Campus
Keep repeating what they said before,
But what with all this football fever
They would like to say a little more –
Bring us back that Rose O' Glory
Pin it to your Cream and Crimson tie,
We'll plant it by the Jordan
Below the towering chimes
Where it will never, ever ever die!

The evening was supposed to end at 10:00 p.m. with the Singing Hoosiers performing in the second half of the evening. Because Stahr and other speakers spoke too long, the Hoosiers performance began late. Coach Pont and the football team walked out along with Hoagy Carmichael and half of the audience. The next song on the program was supposed to be "Stardust." The Singing Hoosiers immediately broke into the

"IU Fight Song" as the team exited the Palladium. The next day more than half of the Singing Hoosiers became ill with food poisoning from the banquet. Despite acute discomfort, the ensemble performed at the halftime show of the UCLA Basketball Classic.

Pont quartered his team Saturday and Sunday at Passionate Father's Retreat in the foothills of the San Gabriel Mountains just outside Pasadena. The monastery complex consisted of sand-colored, adobe-style, two-story buildings populated with monks wearing cassocks with brown hoods and rope belts. They flitted about in silence. Each team member was assigned a separate room with a single cot. Players were free to enjoy leisurely strolls through the orange groves and other bounties of the temperate Southern California climate.

No one regretted the relocation more than Terry Cole. Cole had encouraged friends and followers to gift him bottles of wine, which he kept on ice in the bathtub at the Sheraton. He and his roommate Jade Butcher had to use their neighbor's shower because their tub was full of wine. When they moved to the monastery, Cole's "spirits" went down the drain.

The Rose Bowl Parade rolled off Monday at noon. Senator Everett McKinley Dirksen was honored as the Grand Marshal. Dirksen began his career as a congressman in 1933 and was serving as minority leader of the US Senate. Dirksen rode at the front of the parade in a rose-covered grand marshal's automobile. Betty White, actress and honorary mayor of Hollywood, and Lorne Greene, star of *Bonanza*, narrated the parade. The IU Marching Hundred, actually numbering 148 musicians, was twelfth in line, followed immediately by the Big Ten official float, which was titled "The Greatest Adventure" and featured IU's cheerleaders and beauty queens. The State of Indiana float, titled "The Four Seasons of Adventure," was unit no. 71. It featured Miss Indiana, Mary Lynn Haglund, skating on a portable ice rink that had roses frozen under the surface. As the float passed the television cameras, it ran over a manhole and lurched forward just enough to knock the beauty queen over in mid-pirouette. She suffered painful lower back injuries. The team skipped the whole affair.

The Rose Bowl was dressed for the ball. The IU end zone was splashed with cream and crimson and the goal posts were painted cream with crimson stripes. The USC end zone sported a gold base with cardinal letters. Their goal posts were gold with cardinal stripes. Even the grass on the sidelines was painted gold. Bansch of the *Indianapolis Star* commented that the field had more decorations than World War II hero Audie Murphy.

Harry Gonso and John Isenbarger at Lawry's Beef Bowl.

Cal Snowden trotted on the field for a walk-through with the team before the game and said to himself, "If I died today I will have lived a full life." He marveled about how few guys have the opportunity to play in a Rose Bowl game. Mike Baughman worked his pregame exercises with just his helmet, no pads. A dead silence in the stadium was broken by thundering drum rolls as USC's band marched into the stadium led by a Trojan on a magnificent white steed. The steed rose up on his hind legs and pawed the air. Baughman looked at special team member Jay Mathias and said, "Oh, God, we're in trouble now."

The Rose Bowl

Miss Indiana, Mary Lynn Haglund, skating in the parade.

IU President Elvis J. Stahr (left) with Senator Everett Dirksen and Rose Bowl Queen Linda Strother.

Much to Isenbarger's disappointment, his oft-rehearsed introduction lines, "John Isenbarger, halfback from Muncie, Indiana," were never requested. NBC-TV, which handled the telecast of the game, substituted taped interviews and film clips of some of the players on their home campuses. Super Bowl

Cinderella Ball

sportscaster Curt Gowdy called the game, and Paul Christman, former Missouri star, provided the color.

At two o'clock in the afternoon, with no sign of LA fog, Indiana captain Doug Crusan met Tim Rossovich and Adrian Young, cocaptains of USC, at the 50-yard line before a capacity crowd of 103,946, the largest attendance in bowl history. They stood with the referees on a painted red rose fifteen feet in diameter as the referee flipped a coin. Crusan won the toss and elected to receive.

Only points scored by IU in Rose Bowl history.

Isenbarger took the opening kickoff from Rossovich and managed to bring the ball out to the Indiana 25-yard line before slipping on the turf. On the first play from scrimmage Gonso ran the option to the left. He also slipped after a gain of about four yards. Indiana picked up a first down on another Gonso keeper around right end. Gonso was freed for extra yards when Isenbarger, who was ahead of the play, turned and executed a perfect crackback block.

Gonso tried a pass to Al Gage that was knocked down and almost intercepted. On third down and eight, Gonso rolled out with three USC defensive men chasing him. He completed a pass for the second first down to Al Gage.

The Rose Bowl

Pankratz and O.J. Simpson at Disneyland.

In the first series, Gonso had been chased all over his backfield by Rossovich. He failed to further advance the ball and called for Isenbarger to punt. Isenbarger kicked the football to the USC 16-yard line where it rolled dead, 43 yards and no return. USC fashioned a drive with passes to their talented end Earl McCullouch, an elite sprinter, and runs by O.J. Simpson. Linebackers Kaczmarek and Sniadecki caught Simpson more than a few times but he was smooth and quick. On one play, Kaczmarek and Cunningham zeroed in on Simpson as he swept around right end. The IU players converged on Simpson but he slipped between them and they collided with each other while Simpson went for a first down. Ernie Plank, IU's defensive coordinator, had prepared his players. He told them that Simpson would find his own daylight and would be difficult to bring down. The first two times Kornowa tried to tackle him, he didn't even touch him. On the twelfth play of the series, USC brought the ball to the IU goal line. Pont sent in Jerry Grecco to support the goal-line stand, but Simpson dove up in the air over a pile of pads and jerseys to score a touchdown. The extra point was good, and the score was 7-0. It was an 84-yard drive over 13 plays.

Cinderella Ball

On Indiana's second possession, Gonso fumbled the ball after a hard hit, giving USC strategic possession at midfield. USC ran a fake to Simpson that caught Indiana flat-footed and picked up 20 yards on a reverse, bringing the ball to the IU 20-yard line.

USC's large offensive linemen continued to have their way. On a pass play Tom Bilunas found himself on a defensive shift maneuver lined up across from behemoth Ron Yary. It was like looking through a door. Max Stultz of the *Indianapolis Star* wrote, "Yary could look in second-story windows in his bare feet." Stultz added, "Fortunately he is harmless—he doesn't eat people—just passes out a few blood clots." Indiana's defensive line was led by their big man Doug Crusan at almost 6'5"; USC had a half-dozen Crusans on their offensive line.

During one rally Pont inserted Bob Moynihan, who hadn't played since breaking his leg early in the season. He had been cleared to practice for a month and Ariail vowed to get him ready to play. Ariail spent an hour elaborately taping Moynihan from his toes all the way up to his crotch. Moynihan called Ariail "coach." Ariail liked that.

At the four-yard line USC picked up a first down. Another USC touchdown looked to be a certainty, but USC fumbled at the goal line. The ball squirted into the end zone, where linebacker Bob Nichols pounced on it. The Ohio native, who had chosen IU over 107 other scholarship offers, was an important component of the linebacker crew. The Hoosiers took over on their own 20-yard line. IU gave the ball back when Stolberg fumbled after a long pass reception on the Trojan five-yard line after he was speared by All-American Mike Battle. After the game, Stolberg began spitting blood and was taken to the hospital with two broken ribs. The first quarter ended USC 7, Indiana 0. Indiana had been unable to cross the midfield stripe.

At the beginning of the second quarter, USC gambled on fourth down and short yardage. The give was to Simpson, who was stopped for no gain, and IU took over at midfield. On third down, a quick kick by Isenbarger was picked up on the six-yard line by Mike Battle and returned all the way to midfield, but there was an offside penalty on the play. Indiana drove to the Trojan 29-yard line before losing possession on downs.

USC failed to move the ball as the IU defense began to dig in. During that series defensive back Dave Kornowa was knocked out cold. He woke up and wandered over to the sideline—the USC sideline—and knelt down. He blacked out again and woke up on his own bench trying to figure out where he was. He said to himself, "Geez, I'm at the Rose Bowl." USC had to kick to the only receiver waiting for the ball, Harry Gonso, who carried to the IU 39-yard line before stopped by Ron Yary. Krivoshia, a workhorse who generally carried for short yardage, brought the ball to the 32-yard line of USC. Steve Applegate, filling in for the hurting Mauro, freed Terry Cole for an eight-yard slash through the line. Gonso, chased along his right sideline by a host of players, threw to Jade Butcher, who was pushed out of bounds on the 10-yard line. Gonso on an option play hit Al Gage right in the letters in the end zone. Gage dropped the ball.

Kornowa watched Gage drop the touchdown pass and thought, "Ok, we're going to kick. He didn't remember who the kicker was for a moment, then realized, "Oh, I think it's me." Pont said to him, "Dave put your string on." Kornowa always tied his toe back with a string around his ankle to achieve better loft on the ball. He put on his string and took his place in the backfield. He said to himself, "Keep your eye on the ball. Just keep your eye on the ball." He executed a perfect 27-yard field goal that could have gone for 50 yards. The score was USC 7, Indiana 3.

On the next series the give was to O. J. Simpson. Nate Cunningham went for a tackle but Simpson was too quick and Cunningham got nothing but air as "The Juice" ran down the line of scrimmage with Cunningham in pursuit. Finding no room, Simpson abruptly turned and started running back the other way, right toward Cunningham. Cunningham went for a tackle and again came up with nothing. Cunningham had missed Simpson twice on the same play. Simpson was finally brought down by Dave Kornowa, whose cerebrum was still not fully engaged. After a missed tackle, a frustrated Pankratz commented to his teammates, "O. J. doesn't try to run over you like Leroy Keyes but more like Ron Johnson of Michigan, he is a slasher and a slider and he can turn on speed at any time which gives him an opportunity to cut either way. If I go one way he goes the other."

Defensive end Tom Bilunas was called for a face mask penalty, which nullified a quarterback sack and gave USC the ball in Indiana territory. Simpson broke a long run and was driven out of bounds by Baughman at the 12-yard line, but a clipping penalty nullified the play. It was the seventh penalty assessed against USC in the first half. Jim Murray of the *Los Angeles Times* called the game play as sloppy as a hippie's hairdo. USC threatened at the 16-yard line with time running out. Kaz called for a blitz. At the snap, Moynihan took a half-step back and fooled his offensive counterpart. Moynihan took off for the quarterback and sacked him for a ten-yard loss to the IU 26-yard line. USC completed a pass on fourth down but it wasn't enough for a first down and Indiana took over on their own 15-yard line.

After IU failed to move the ball, Isenbarger kicked to Mike Battle, who ran it back to midfield. USC called time out with 12 seconds left. Their last play was a long pass that was intercepted by Nate Cunningham. The half ended with the score 7-3 in favor of USC.

IU fans were not disappointed that their team had fallen behind at halftime. In fact, many would have been surprised had Indiana gone into the locker room leading USC. Indiana was a comeback fourth-quarter team, and they were only one score away from beating USC. Most fans stayed in their seats to enjoy the halftime presentation, "Adventures in Hoosier Land" featuring the IU Marching Hundred band. The show featured a salute to alumnus Hoagy Carmichael, who was in the stands that day. The band played his immortal "Stardust," music he wrote while a student at Indiana. The presentation also included "Back Home Again in Indiana" and Meredith Willson's "76 Trombones" as the band recognized Elkhart, Indiana, the world's largest band instrument manufacturing center. During that number, the Hoosier Hundred formed a huge slide trombone on the field. The band then saluted Indiana-born Cole Porter with the playing of Porter's "Night and Day." It seemed like night and day for the band, as they had already marched in their new uniforms in the Rose Bowl Parade that morning. The uniforms were black with long tailcoats and white fronts. Across the front "Indiana" was written in red block letters. An IU monogram adorned the back of the coat.

The Hoosier Hundred moved from the geometric design into one of an auto race track to recognize the Indianapolis 500 Memorial Day auto classic. Three miniature race cars, painted in the colors of Purdue University, the University of Notre Dame, and IU, circled the track as the band played "Can Can" and "Indiana, Our Indiana." The band's concert selections, saluting not only the Hoosier State but the entire United States, were "This Land Is My Land" and "This Is My Country." They played "Auld Lang Syne" as they marched off the field.

Simpson sparked the Trojans in the second half with a kickoff return of 28 yards. Mike Deal, a strapping 6'3" defensive back from Hobart, Indiana, played second man in from the left on the kickoff team. He was instructed to stay in his lane but when the kickoff went to the opposite side of the field, Deal cut straight across the field and got to Simpson just in time for a "JOP." A "JOP" is a "Jump on the Pile," an opportunity to have one's number in front of the TV camera for the folks back home. USC was unable to sustain a drive on their first possession and kicked to Indiana. Gage, anxious to make amends for his drop, caught a seven-yard pass from Gonso at the Indiana 24. Isenbarger picked up the first down on a 14-yard run after a pitch from Gonso. Gonso was stopped on a keeper by the only USC defender between him and the goal line. A Gonso pass was batted down by defensive end Mike

Hayhoe, a 6'8" senior who replaced Jim Gunn at left end for USC. IU had to punt. Gunn had great speed, but he suffered torn ligaments during the UCLA game and was unable to play in the Rose Bowl. Coach McKay commented, "Gunn could catch their quarterback, Harry Gonso. Hayhoe couldn't catch me." Hayhoe did block two field goal attempts by UCLA.

Simpson sat out the next four plays after a hard hit by Kevin Duffy, but he had plenty of "Juice" left. On the first play after he returned, he ran for seven yards. On a halfback option, Simpson overthrew receiver Ron Drake, who was waiting unmolested just outside the end zone. On fourth down from the 19-yard line, USC attempted a field goal. It was wide to the left. Indiana failed to take advantage of its good fortune and gave the ball back to USC with good field position at the Indiana 45-yard line. With little over three minutes left in the third quarter, Simpson took the ball up the middle to the 14-yard line through a huge Yary hole. Simpson scored from the eight-yard line for his second touchdown, breaking two tackles along the way.

On the last play of the third quarter, Gonso connected again with Gage. The third quarter ended with the score USC 14, IU 3. IU threatened in the fourth quarter with help by a pass interference call on a pass to Eric Stolberg, who was playing through his pain. On the thirteenth play of the series, Gonso had to leave the field with a muscle spasm in his leg after he was kicked on third down just slightly short of the first-down marker. The referees paused to measure and called the ball just inches shy. Mike Perry ran into the huddle with no time to warm up or prepare. He tried Cole through the middle for a loss then he called another running play with both backs on the left side of the line. Monk looked up and said, "Redbird we don't even have that play." Butcher said, "Just throw me an out." Perry overthrew Butcher, and the ball went over to USC with eleven minutes left in the game.

Inspired defense by Indiana threw Simpson for a loss two times in that possession, forcing USC to kick the ball back to

The Rose Bowl

Indiana. Butcher returned a booming 47-yard punt 20 yards. Gage caught a 16-yard Gonso toss into USC territory for a first down. The IU dream was still alive. With a little more than four minutes left in the game and still trailing 14-3, IU had a fourth-down situation. Gonso threw a desperate pass that was grabbed out of the air by Jade Butcher, giving Indiana four more downs. Indiana advanced the ball to third and one but suffered an illegal procedure penalty. On fourth and six, Gonso was caught behind the line of scrimmage by tackle Gary Magner for a 10-yard loss that gave the ball back to USC with less than four minutes to play. The game ended 14-3 as neither team could score in the fourth quarter. After the game USC students paraded out to midfield carrying signs reading "It's Midnight, Cinderella."

O. J. Simpson carried 25 times for 128 yards and was named "Player of the Game" by the Helms Athletic Foundation. He credited his offensive line. "Our line was great," he said. "It opened some real big holes out there." He called Indiana, "a real fine football team" and added, "They were just as tough as I thought they would be." McKay gave Indiana its due. Standing on a bench in his locker room and puffing a cigar he said, "I thought Indiana was a very fine football team."

As the IU team entered the locker room, Jerry Grecco delivered a vicious kick to the locker room door. Standing on top of an equipment trunk, the 5'6" Pont told players, coaches, press, and all alumni who managed to cram in that he had no kicks. His team was extremely disappointed but they knew they were playing a good club. He vowed that IU would return to the Rose Bowl. President Stahr answered press inquiries with, "I'm proud of them. They fought hard and they never gave up."

Grecco pulled his roommate and close friend Tom Bilunas aside and whispered, "I sent myself in the game."

Bilunas didn't understand, "You what?"

"Well, I was on the sidelines and I said to myself, 'You didn't come all the way to the Rose Bowl just to watch.' I just couldn't stand it anymore. I ran in and tapped Wolfer (Bill Wolfe).

Believe me, the game is more exciting from the field."

Late that night Moynihan walked into his room and spied his roommate, Dave Kornowa, on the edge of the bed. Kornowa was subdued and said, "Is the game over?"

Moynihan replied, "Yeah, yeah."

"Did we win?"

"No, we didn't win, Dave."

"What was the score?"

"14-3."

"How'd we get the three points?"

"Well, you kicked a field goal in the first quarter, Dave."

Kornowa's football career was over. He kicked himself into Hoosier history as the only Rose Bowl point-scoring player in the history of the school. His kicks also provided the winning margins against Kansas (18-15) and Michigan State (14-13). According to Warren Ariail, "He did it all with a right leg that has a knee held together by piano wire. He is one of the toughest kids we have."

Earlier that evening, John Isenbarger was a dinner guest at the home of Tom Harmon, former All-American halfback who once tried to recruit him for his alma mater, Michigan. "I had a great time," Isenbarger said. "I was in his trophy room. He has a few nice little items like a Heisman Trophy."

Kaz was scheduled to leave the next day for the Hula Bowl, and equipment manager Red Grow helped him pack his gear. Grow was a counselor and friend to coaches and student athletes alike. Grow stopped and said, "You can't take a helmet like this to the Hula Bowl." The steel face mask was visibly bent at least a half an inch.

Wednesday afternoon on the plane home to Indiana, Pont thought back to the beginning of the 1967 season. He remembered thinking that one play, one moment, could have made a difference in the final score in most of the games played in 1965 and 1966, his first two years at the helm. He thought about the game his team had played Monday and listed those moments: a dropped pass in the end zone by one of his best receivers, Al Gage, who gave a stellar performance in the Rose Bowl nonetheless; failure to convert a first down with two plays and inches to go with Harry Gonso on the sidelines with a muscle spasm; a fumble on the USC five-yard line caused by a vicious spearing tackle—a technique that should be outlawed—after a brilliant catch by Eric Stolberg; the loss of right tackle Bob Kirk, whose presence on the line may have allowed Gonso a few seconds more—all he needed—to complete his hookups with Stolberg, Gage, Butcher, and Isenbarger.

Waiting for the team when they returned to Indiana University on Wednesday was a welcome home rally in the IU fieldhouse. The theme "We Shall Return" was echoed by President Stahr, Chancellor Wells, and Coach Pont. Bob Russell, who had played his last football game for Indiana University in the Rose Bowl, summarized the game:

> I had three experiences at Pasadena that really made an impression on me and I think will stay with me the rest of my life. The day before the game Coach Pont took us to the Rose Bowl and we went up the elevator to the press box. When I looked out from there and saw those big red letters in the white end zone spelling Indiana I tell you it was a terrific experience. It was the first time I really realized we were in the Rose Bowl. Then the next day, when we ran out of the locker room into the tunnel and the Marching 100 was there playing the school song. I went on that field running about three feet off the ground. And when we got out there, the whole west side of the stadium was a sea of red and white pompom shakers. I said, "Look at that!" and so did some other guys. It was just a tremendous experience. I don't think I'll ever forget what Indiana University has done for me.

Coach Pont followed Russell to the dais and was introduced to cheers that took more than a minute to subside. After announcing that Russell had been admitted to Indiana University Medical School, he asked the team to stand together for the last time.

President Stahr said, "IU has never been so well represented as it was in California. The university celebrates its sesquicentennial in 1970. We intend to start off that wonderful year by playing again in California." Curt Simic, assistant director of the Indiana University Foundation, was master of ceremonies. Other speakers were *Indiana Daily Student* sports editor Rick Roth, athletic director Bill Orwig, and Bloomington mayor John Hooker. Simic called the team the most exciting team in college football. Stahr told the throng that Rose Bowl Tournament officials who had been sponsoring the event for decades said they had "never been so impressed by those on the gridiron and fans of any school in competition there as they were with IU."

The cheerleaders led the crowd in the school song to end the reception as Pont vowed, "We shall return."

EPILOGUE

John Pont never returned.

The Big Ten no-repeat rule restricted Indiana from the Rose Bowl until 1969, and the 1968 team wasn't in contention anyway, since they finished the conference schedule at 4-3. Indiana opened the 1969 season with a 3-1 record in Big Ten play, including a 16-0 shutout over Michigan State. The schedule favored IU with soft opponents Iowa and Northwestern yet to play. Fans were buoyed by the possibility of another trip to Pasadena, but there was another more dire possibility, and the coaches didn't see it coming.

The 1969 team was a product of the times—and the times were changing. Just a few years prior, in 1964, the Civil Rights Act was enacted and Cassius Clay dropped his "slave name" in favor of Muhammad Ali, sending a message of racial pride to African Americans. There were race riots in July of 1967 in Detroit and Newark. That summer, the IU Board of Trustees adopted resolutions directing the university administration to take necessary steps to remove every vestige of discrimination based on race, creed, or national origin. Despite these actions, bigotry and hatred could not be legislated away, and some players on the 1969 team felt it existed in their midst.

Student body president Ted Najam warned that student unrest was brewing at Indiana University. He wrote in 1968, "It cannot be ignored or written off as a sporadic phenomenon, though some people seem remarkably secure in an 'It can't happen here' attitude. Neither will it be silenced by harsh treatment of student dissenters; this kind of half-solution only serves to exacerbate the situation which then expands as it feeds on itself."

Almost all the players in 1967, black and white, felt Pont's best players always played. The feeling was different in 1969. A few influential black team members, bolstered by the emerging black pride of national events, spoke up about their perception of being treated as second-class citizens. They took issue with the concept of coaches stacking black players so they would be competing against each other instead of starting at other positions.

In a sudden action that surprised Pont, fourteen African American players who felt that their grievances about racial issues had not been properly addressed did not report to practice. Pont and his coaches met with the players and allowed them to return to practice with no penalty. Only four accepted Pont's offer. Among those who did not return were seniors Clarence Price and Benny Norman, sometimes starters during the 1967 season. The team, riddled with the absences of ten significant contributors, lost all their remaining games. The boycott issue made it difficult for Pont to recruit talented players, especially African Americans, for years to come. The Hoosier dream was over for John Pont, who left in 1972 to coach Northwestern. He died in 2008 at the age of eighty. The black boycott of 1969 is a tragic footnote to the extraordinary 1967 season and the promise of winning football in Bloomington.

Bill Orwig arrived as Indiana University's athletic director during the dark days of IU probation. During Orwig's fifteen years, the Hoosiers won thirty-seven Big Ten championships in seven sports and six NCAA titles. Home football attendance averaged 25,854 the year before Orwig arrived, and by 1969 it had more than doubled to 53,319. Orwig also guided the expansion of the school's athletic facilities, including the Assembly Hall basketball facility. He retired in 1975 with his dream of a long tradition of winning football all but abandoned. Orwig was inducted into the University of Michigan Athletic Hall of Honor in 1984 and the Indiana University Hall of Fame in 1987. He died of cancer on July 30, 1994, at the age of eighty-six.

Harry Gonso quarterbacked two more IU teams but never again competed for the Big Ten championship. In fact, the Old Oaken Bucket stayed in West Lafayette during the rest of Gonso's reign. Gonso received his Bachelor of Science degree from Indiana University–Bloomington in 1970 as an Academic All-American and All–Big Ten selection. Although he regretted his inability to win consistently for his beloved coach in 1968 and 1969, he did accomplish a major personal goal, a law degree. He earned his juris doctorate from the Indiana University School of Law, where he graduated with honors in 1973. Gonso joined the law firm of Ice Miller in 1980. He retired on January 10, 2005, to serve Indiana governor Mitch Daniels as senior counsel and chief of staff during 2005 and 2006 and rejoined the firm in December 2006. Indiana governors Bowen, Orr, and Daniels bestowed the Sagamore of the Wabash on Gonso, one of the highest honors accorded by the state of Indiana.

Many of the starters on the 1967 team earned all-star honors including All-American, All–Big Ten, and induction in the IU Hall of Fame. Some enjoyed successful NFL careers. Captain Doug Crusan was drafted by the Miami Dolphins in the first round and played with IU teammate Terry Cole on the only undefeated team in NFL history. Cole was runner-up for Rookie of the Year in 1968 when he was with the Baltimore Colts. Eric Stolberg suited up for the New England Patriots for most of one season. John Isenbarger played for the San Francisco 49ers for four years before opting for Hawaii in the World Football

League. Jim Sniadecki also played for the 49ers. He enjoyed five years. Cal Snowden spent five seasons with the St. Louis Cardinals, the Buffalo Bills, and the San Diego Chargers. Don Warner had a stint with the Dallas Cowboys, and Mike Krivoshia played two years with the Houston Oilers.

Many chose coaching as a career. Harold Mauro and Nate Cunningham had the privilege of coaching with John Pont. Almost everyone enjoyed fulfilling lives after graduating IU. Many credited lessons learned on the gridiron—lessons of cooperation, team play, discipline, and pride.

In addition to regular reunions, the team has connected in a special way. Almost every member of the team contributed to the Rose Bowl and the John Pont scholarship funds. Eric Stolberg established the Terry P. Cole memorial scholarship in honor of his friend who succumbed to cancer in 2005. Ken Kaczmarek and his wife, Linda, established a scholarship, as did David Evans and his wife Rae.

At the forty-fifth reunion the team planted a tree in front of Memorial Stadium with a plaque designating the tree as the 1967 Big Ten champions and 1968 Rose Bowl tree.

The 1967 team captured the imagination and recaptured football glory for Indiana for one brilliant moment in history. It was a team that always thought they could win, and they won with reckless panache. In eight of the ten games, IU played the last four minutes with the game in the balance. They won them all. Fifty years have elapsed since that first day of practice on September 1, 1967—fifty years and not one Big Ten championship or Rose Bowl appearance.

Why was the 1967 team so successful? Historians and statisticians offer reasons. The Big Ten was weak. The combined record of teams IU defeated, not including Purdue, was 22-55-3. A formidable Ohio State team wasn't even on the schedule. Many of these opponents beat themselves with unaccountable blunders, such as tripping a team member on the way to an unobstructed touchdown or throwing wildly at a receiver standing unguarded in the end zone waiting for the game-winning reception. An abundance of good luck favored the team. Tipped balls and fumbles seemed to fall in the right hands. The defense benefited by having a solid, unheralded group of upperclassmen linebackers and interior linemen that kept the score close enough for the team's last-minute heroics. The coach, more savvy than most of his colleagues, provided a strategic edge.

But those who were there, those who suited up, know the real answer. They won because their 1967 team was a family. Like all families, there were quarrels and controversies, but real friendships were forged. The team played with and for each other. They refused to be intimidated; they played with swagger and confidence—together. Like their song goes, they had the whole world in their hands.

* * *

INTERVIEWS

Applegate, Steve (Plug), center, Cincinnati, Ohio, December 12, 2016.

Baughman, Mike, safety, Lancaster, Ohio, November 30, 2016.

Bilunas, Tom, defensive end, Gary, Indiana, December 12, 2016.

Butcher, Jade, flanker, Bloomington, Indiana, October 4, 2016.

Crusan, Doug, defensive tackle, Monessen, Pennsylvania, September 26, 2016.

Cunningham, Nate, defensive halfback, Danville, Illinois, October 13, 2016.

Doninger, Clarence, IU athletic director 1991–2001, August 3, 2016.

Duffy, Kevin, linebacker, Hartford, Connecticut, November 8, 2016, and December 12, 2016.

Gage, Al, tight end, East Saint Louis, Illinois, October 6, 2016.

Gill, Cordell, defensive end, Washington, DC, December 16, 2016.

Gonso, Harry, quarterback, Findlay, Ohio, July 6, 2016, and September 21, 2016.

Hackney, Carol, sister of Terry Cole, October 8, 2016.

Isenbarger, John (Iso), halfback, Muncie, Indiana, October 26, 2016.

Kaczmarek, Ken (Kaz), linebacker, South Bend, Indiana, August 31, 2016.

Kirk, Bob, tackle, Bloomington, Indiana, October 24, 2016.

Kleinschmidt, Dean, student trainer, Morgan, Minnesota, October 5, 2016.

Kornowa, Dave, defensive halfback/kicker, Toledo, Ohio, November 8, 2016.

Levy, Morris (Blondie), student manager, October 18, 2016.

Mauro, Harold (Monk), center, Verona, Pennsylvania, October 17, 2016.

Moynihan, Bob, linebacker, Hammond, Indiana, December 29, 2016.

Mourouzis, Nick, assistant coach, Uhrichsville, Ohio, November 14, 2016.

Orwig, Bill, Jr., son of IU athletic director Bill Orwig, August 8, 2016.

Pankratz, Karl, linebacker, Toledo, Ohio, October 10, 2016, and November 20, 2016.

Perry, Mike (Redbird), quarterback, Indianapolis, Indiana, November 9, 2016.

Smulyan, Jeff, USC student/writer for *Indianapolis Star*, Indianapolis, Indiana, January 13, 2017.

Snowden, Cal, defensive end, Washington, DC, November 1, 2016.

Stolberg, Eric, split end, Cuyahoga Falls, Ohio, October 13, 2016.

Tuchman, Steve, cochair, Student Rose Bowl Committee, December 29, 2016.

Interviews

Warner, Don (Donny), kicker, Gary, Indiana, January 17, 2017.

White, Eugene, guard, South Bend, Indiana, January 5, 2017.

SOURCES

Descriptions of weather conditions in the Bloomington area throughout the book are drawn from daily Cooperative Observers meteorological records taken at various stations around Bloomington and reported to the US Weather Bureau and from the *Indianapolis Star* weather reports.

1968 Rose Bowl, Indiana vs. USC (www.youtube.com).

"10,000 Fans Can't Be Wrong, Roses Smell Sweet." *Indiana Daily Student*, November 28, 1967.

"Another IU Critic Eats Crow, Also." *Herald-Times* (Indiana), November 28, 1967.

Arnold, Robert D. *The Rivalry.* Bloomington, IN: AuthorHouse, 2009.

Arnold, Robert D. *A Team of Destiny: The Unforgettable Story of Indiana's 1967 Big Ten Championship Season And the Rose Bowl of 1968.* Bloomington, IN: AuthorHouse, 2011.

B. J. "Stolberg's 'Harnessing' Pain." *Indianapolis Star*, December 31, 1967.

Baird, Weldon. "Guard Bob Russell Admires Coach Pont." *Indiana Daily Student*, December 1, 1967.

Balough, Richard. "Warmath Says IU's Fine Team." *Herald-Times* (Indiana), November 19, 1967.

Balough, Richard. "Hoosiers Get Send-Off." *Herald-Times* (Indiana), December 20, 1967.

Bansch, John. "Pont Puts I.U. 'Kids' on Stage." *Indianapolis Star*, May 12, 1967.

Bansch, John. "Isenbarger Cream of I.U. Crop." *Indianapolis Star*, May 14, 1967.

Bansch, John. "Mich. State on Brink of Big Ten Record." *Indianapolis Star*, September 2, 1967.

Bansch, John. "State's 'Big Three' Start Grid Campaign." *Indianapolis Star*, September 23, 1967.

Bansch, John. "Cole Improved; Pressure Is Off." *Indianapolis Star*, October 3, 1967.

Bansch, John. "Hoosier Grid Task Only Half Learned." *Indianapolis Star*, October 11, 1967.

Bansch, John. "Juggling John's Theories." *Indianapolis Star*, October 24, 1967.

Bansch, John. "Odd Couple at I.U. Guard Berths." *Indianapolis Star*, October 26, 1967.

Bansch, John. "IU Thrill Show Goes West Tonight." *Indianapolis Star*, October 28, 1967.

Bansch, John. "This Butcher Has Hands of Surgeon." *Indianapolis Star*, October 31, 1967.

Bansch, John. "Gonso's OK, Hoosiers Go for 7th KO." *Indianapolis Star*, November 4, 1967.

Bansch, John. "I.U. Escape Artists Make It No. 7." *Indianapolis Star*, November 5, 1967.

Bansch, John. "Pont Treats 'Loose Kids.'" *Indianapolis Star*, November 6, 1967.

Bansch, John. "Big 10 Title Drama Unfolds Today." *Indianapolis Star*, November 11, 1967.

Sources

Bansch, John. "Bowl Talk Is No Longer Forbidden in I.U. Camp." *Indianapolis Star*, November 14, 1967.

Bansch, John. "Indiana's Progress Can Be 'Gaged' By Star." *Indianapolis Star*, November 15, 1967.

Bansch, John. "Hoosiers Out to Rout Gophers in Rose Bed." *Indianapolis Star*, November 18, 1967.

Bansch, John. "9-1? Even Pont Surprised." *Indianapolis Star*, November 19, 1967.

Bansch, John. "No Defeatism in I.U. Camp." *Indianapolis Star*, November 21, 1967.

Bansch, John. "I.U. Hones Defense for Purdue." *Indianapolis Star*, November 22, 1967.

Bansch, John. "Punting John Has Serious Side." *Indianapolis Star*, November 23, 1967.

Bansch, John. "O.J. Would Prefer Gophers to I.U.'s Speedy Chasers." *Indianapolis Star*, November 24, 1967.

Bansch, John. "A Bucket Game with Meaning." *Indianapolis Star*, November 25, 1967.

Bansch, John. "Hoosiers to Face Southern Cal; Upset Boilermakers for 3-Way Tie." *Indianapolis Star*, November 26, 1967.

Bansch, John. "Veni, Vidi, Vici! West-Roamin' Hoosiers Feted." *Indianapolis Star*, November 29, 1967.

Bansch, John. "Students Honor I.U. Gridders." *Indianapolis Star*, December 20, 1967.

Bansch, John. "Hoosier Outfit Hit Drills Early." *Indianapolis Star*, December 22, 1967.

Bansch, John. "Doug Crusan Ready to Make Another Sacrifice for I.U." *Indianapolis Star*, December 23, 1967.

Bansch, John. "Hoosiers Down to Game Week." *Indianapolis Star*, December 25, 1967.

Bansch, John. "Indiana Mixing 'Boilermaker' for USC." *Indianapolis Star*, December 29, 1967.

Bansch, John. "Happy Hooligans Hit on Schedule." *Indianapolis Star*, December 30, 1967.

Bansch, John. "QB's Dream Brings I.U. Roses." *Indianapolis Star*, December 31, 1967.

Bansch, John. "I.U. Could be Highest Rated TV Attraction." *Indianapolis Star*, December 31, 1967.

Bansch, John. "Hoosier Hearts Are Sad but Heads High." *Indianapolis Star*, January 3, 1968.

Berke, Art. "I.U. Gets Fair Shake." *Indiana Daily Student*, November 10, 1967.

Berkow, Ira. "IU Snaps 82-Year Slump; Sophs Lauded," *Herald-Times* (Indiana), November 12, 1967.

Berry, Jack. "Spartans Gird for 'Playoff.'" *Detroit Free Press*, October 20, 1967.

Biggs, Pat. "Pont Calls Win 'Step Forward.'" *Courier-Journal* (Louisville), September 24, 1967.

Bliven, Bruce, Jr. "The Professor and the Toothpaste" (undated and unpublished treatise) New York.

Burgess, Dale. "Time Runs Out on UW; Indiana Posts 14-9 Win." *Green Bay Press*, November 5, 1967.

C. J. Jr. "No. 1 Fan Proud of I.U. Rose Battle." *Indianapolis Star*, January 2, 1968.

Cadou, Jep, Jr. "Miss Indiana's Tumble Highlights Rose Parade." *Indianapolis Star*, January 2, 1968.

Capshew, James H. "Alma Pater: Herman B Wells and the Rise of Indiana University," Indiana.edu/-wells/index.php/archive/the-man-himself/stories/168-story-alma-pater.html.

Chamberlain, Charles. "Big 10 Unbeaten Clubs Look to Fatten Records Against Weaker Rivals." Post-Crescent (Wisconsin), November 3, 1967.

Sources

Chamberlain, Charles. "Hoosiers Are Favored by 3 over Gophers." *Manitowoc Herald-Times*, November 14, 1967.

Chamberlain, Charles. "Win over Gophers Vital to Hoosiers." *Manitowoc Herald-Times*, November 17, 1967.

Chapin, Dwight. "Confident Gonso Chose Indiana over Michigan State—Honest!" *Los Angeles Times*, December 27, 1967.

Clark, Dr. Thomas D. "Kinsey and the Kinsey Institute" (transcript of interview of Dr. Herman B Wells), Bloomington, IN, January 1968.

Collier, Warren. "Amazing IU 'Kids' Top Purdue, Head for Bowl." *Muncie Star*, November 27, 1967.

Collins, Bob. "Sports Over Lightly." *Indianapolis Star*, September 24, 1967.

Collins, Bob. "'67 May be I.U. Comeback Year." *Indianapolis Star*, September 25, 1967.

Collins, Bob. "Sports Over Lightly." *Indianapolis Star*, October 1, 1967.

Collins, Bob. "Sports Over Lightly." *Indianapolis Star*, October 11, 1967.

Collins, Bob. "Sports Over Lightly." *Indianapolis Star*, October 15, 1967.

Collins, Bob. "Storm-Tossed I.U. Escapes 5th Time." *Indianapolis Star*, October 22, 1967.

Collins, Bob. "Sports Over Lightly." *Indianapolis Star*, October 22, 1967.

Collins, Bob. "Overconfidence Worrying Unbeaten I.U." *Indianapolis Star*, October 23, 1967.

Collins, Bob. "Sports Over Lightly." *Indianapolis Star*, November 1, 1967.

Collins, Bob. "Sports Over Lightly." *Indianapolis Star*, November 7, 1967.

Collins, Bob. "Sports Over Lightly." *Indianapolis Star*, November 14, 1967.

Collins, Bob. "Sports Over Lightly." *Indianapolis Star*, November 19, 1967.

Collins, Bob. "Sports Over Lightly." *Indianapolis Star*, November 25, 1967.

Collins, Bob. "$499 Goes A-Flyin' – Punt, John." *Indianapolis Star*, December 30, 1967.

Collins, Bob. "Sports Over Lightly." *Indianapolis Star*, December 31, 1967.

Collins, Bob. "Sports Over Lightly." *Indianapolis Star*, January 1, 1968.

Collins, Bob. "Sports Over Lightly." *Indianapolis Star*, January 2, 1968.

"Council Behind I.U. Team." *Herald-Times* (Indiana), November 26, 1967.

Darier, Roy. "Duffy Won't Name Them But Ara Does." *Chicago Tribune*, October 25, 1967.

Dawson, Greg. "We Still Love You, Hoosiers." *Herald-Times* (Indiana), November 19, 1967.

Dawson, Jim. "Soph Quarterbacks Keep Hoosier Foes Honest on Defense." *Tucson Daily Citizen*, October 25, 1967.

Dawson, Jim. "Tom Nelson, Klahr Working on Offense." *Tucson Daily Citizen*, October 25, 1967.

"Defense Praised by I.U.'s Pont." *Herald-Times* (Indiana), November 17, 1967.

"Defense Stars Big Men, Too, at Indiana U." *Lansing State Journal*, November 8, 1967.

Editorial, "Time to Rhyme O'er IU Climb." *Daily Herald-Telephone* (Indiana), November 16, 1967.

Editorial, "Keep the Big Red Ball Rolling." *Indiana Daily Student*, November 28, 1967.

Sources

Editorial, "Blame Pont When He Deserves It." *Indiana Daily Student*, November 30, 1966.

Esper, Dwain. "O.J. Too Much for Hoosiers." *Independent* (California), January 2, 1968.

Fenlon, Dick. "Indiana Does About Face, Rallies to Trip UK 12-10." *Courier-Journal & Times* (Louisville), September 24, 1967.

"Fightin' Hoosiers to get Full Backup Treatment." *Indianapolis Star* (Indiana), December 24, 1967.

Fineman, Alex. "Hayes Produced Champions, Controversy." ESPN Classic SportsCentury Biography (http://www.espn.com/classic/biography/s/Hayes_Woody.html).

Fisher, Roland, "The History of the Indiana University Singing Hoosiers Choral Ensemble." Dissertation submitted to the College of Music of Florida State University.

"Float Drive Started, 'Package' on I.U. Bowl Trip Announced." *Indianapolis Star*, November 27, 1967.

Fox, Janet. "SAB Urges Student Demonstration with Signs, Banners and Roses." *Indiana Daily Student*, December 12, 1967.

Fox, Janet. "Hoosiers Invade the Land of O. J. Simpson." *Indiana Daily Student*, January 5, 1968.

Getz, Bob. "Howard Cosell Makes a Retreat; Well . . . Sort of." *Herald-Times* (Indiana), November 28, 1967.

Goldstein, Richard. "John Pont, Who Coached Indiana to Rose Bowl, Dies at 80." *New York Times*, July 3, 2008.

"Gonso Works Out, Set for Wisconsin Game." *Indianapolis Star*, November 3, 1967.

Grady, Al. "Al Grady's Column." *Iowa City Press*, October 16, 1967.

Hall, John. "Cinderella Lost Slipper, but Didn't Turn into Pumpkin." *Los Angeles Times*, January 2, 1968.

Hamelin, Joe. "Go-Go(nso) Hoosiers Picked to Click by 6." *Indianapolis Star*, September 30, 1967.

Hamelin, Joe. "And I.U. Gridders Don't Shave Yet!" *Indianapolis Star*, November 12, 1967.

Hamelin, Joe. "Purdue's Ears Tuned to I.U." *Indianapolis Star*, November 19, 1967.

Hammel, Bob. "Gary On, Iso Next." *Herald-Times* (Indiana), 1967.

Hammel, Bob. "Just Wait till these Kids Start Shaving." *Herald-Times* (Indiana), November 12, 1967.

Hammel, Bob. "I Bet They Went Crazy Back Home." *Herald-Times* (Indiana), November 12, 1967.

Hammel, Bob. "Everybody Knows What This One Means." *Daily Herald-Telephone* (Indiana), November 13, 1967.

Hammel, Bob. "Who's N-Nervous? Hoosiers 'Little TOO Loose.'" *Daily Herald-Telephone* (Indiana), November 15, 1967.

Hammel, Bob. "Russell, Cassells—IU's All-American Pair." *Daily Herald-Telephone* (Indiana), November 16, 1967.

Hammel, Bob. "A Busy Day," *Indiana Daily Student*, November 23, 1966.

Hammel, Bob. "Pont Finding Fame Fun." *Herald-Times*, December 3, 1967.

Hammel, Bob. "Pont Writers' Coach of Year . . . Of Course," *Daily Herald-Telephone* (Indiana), December 6, 1967.

Hammel, Bob. "Says Captain Doug Crusan, IU Won't Get Out of Shape." *Herald-Times* (Indiana), December 10, 1967.

Hammel, Bob. "Kirk Loss Starts Hunt." *Herald-Times* (Indiana), December 19, 1967.

Hammel, Bob. "Cinder-fella." *Herald-Times* (Indiana), December 29, 1967.

Hammel, Bob. "Pont Doesn't Want Change; USC Hurting." *Daily Herald-Telephone* (Indiana), December 30, 1967.

Hammel, Bob. "IU Begins Its Retreat Today." *Daily Herald-Telephone* (Indiana), December 30, 1967.

Sources

Hammel, Bob. "IU Falters at Key Spots in Rose Bowl Loss." *Daily Herald-Telephone* (Indiana), January 2, 1968.

Hammel, Bob. "Duffy, Kornowa Success Stories At IU." *Daily Herald-Telephone* (Indiana), January 3, 1968.

Hammel, Bob. "Hoosiers Hear Last Hurrahs." *Daily Herald-Telephone* (Indiana), January 4, 1968.

Hammel, Bob. "IU Dominance Coincides with Orwig's Reign." *Herald-Times* (Indiana), February 1971.

Hammel, Bob. "IU's Orwig to Retire Next June." *Daily Herald-Telephone* (Indiana), July 10, 1974.

Hammel, Bob. "Orwig Hoping to Stay on after 65." *Herald-Times* (Indiana), January 28, 1996.

Hammel, Bob, and Kit Klingelhoffer. *Glory of Old IU: 100 Years of Indiana Athletics*. Bloomington, IN: Sports Publishing, 1999.

"Handley to be emcee at Big Ten banquet." *Indiana Daily Student* (Indiana). December 20, 1967.

Hanes, Curt. "Spartan Fight Song Brings Tears to Eye of No. 1 Fan." *Lansing State Journal*, October 8, 1967.

HeraldTimesOnline.com. "IU's previous Nobel Laureates," (http://www.heraldtimesonline.com/stories/2009/10/12/news.qp-7434993.sto?), October 13, 2009.

Hersey, Mark D. "Year of the Pigskin." University of Kansas, Department of History. November 18, 1968 (http://kuhistory.com/articles/year-of-the-pigskin).

Hoerner, Bob. "No Predictions, But Some Hints." *Lansing State Journal*, October 20, 1967.

Hoerner, Bob. "Hot Hoosiers Headed Here." *Lansing State Journal*, November 8, 1967.

Hoerner, Bob. "State Has 'Nothing to Lose' Saturday." *Lansing State Journal*, November 10, 1967.

Hoerner, Bob. "Amazing Hoosiers Hurdle State, 14-13." *Lansing State Journal*, November 12, 1967.

Hoerner, Bob. "Hustle Pays for Indiana." *Lansing State Journal*, November 12, 1967.

"Hoosier Gridders Bigger, Speedier; Pont Has Eyes on 'Break-Even' Year." *Indianapolis Star*, September 2, 1967.

"Hoosiers 'Try Out' UA Lights." *Tucson Daily Citizen*, October 27, 1967.

Hunter, Bob. "Indiana: Rags to Roses and Back." *Los Angeles Herald-Examiner*, January 2, 1968.

"Index Favors Indiana by Six Points." *Tucson Daily Citizen*, October 25, 1967.

"Indiana Among Seven on Undefeated List." *Indianapolis Star*, November 2, 1967.

Indiana Football Hall of Fame. Howard K. Brown (deceased).

Indiana University, official play-by-play report, dressing room quotes and official programs, 1967.

Indiana University. "A Magical Season: 40 Years Later, IU Honors the Cardiac Kids." November 14, 2007. http://iuhoosiers.com/news/2007/11/14/A_Magical_Season_40_Years_Later_IU_Honors_the_Cardiac_Kids.aspx.

Indiana University. "The Singing Hoosiers." Rose Bowl Press Fact Sheet, December 1967.

Indiana University. "Rose Bowl Band Show." Rose Bowl Press Fact Sheet, December 1967.

Inman, Julia. "Rose Bowl Sets TV Color Splash." *Indianapolis Star*, December 24, 1967.

"I.U. Hopes to Upset Duffy as Well as Favored State." *Indiana Daily Student*, November 9, 1967.

"IU to Leave for Coast Thursday." *Daily Herald-Telephone* (Indiana), December 20, 1967.

"IU Won't Make Federal Case of Smog: Ariail." *Daily Herald-Telephone* (Indiana), December 29, 1967.

"IU Will Return, Pont Vows." *Indianapolis Star*, January 2, 1968.

Jenkins, Dan. "Punt, John, Punt!" *Sports Illustrated*, November 13, 1967.

"Kaczmarek Has that Killer Instinct." *Daily Herald-Telephone* (Indiana), 1967.

Kindred, Dave. "UK vs. Indiana: Anything Could Happen." *Courier-Journal* (Louisville), September 23, 1967.

Kinsey, Alfred C. "The Institute for Sex Research." Undated report of the trustees, Paul H. Gebhard, Wardell B. Pomeroy, Cornelia V. Christenson, John H. Gagnon, Theodore W. Torrey, Bloomington, Indiana.

Knight, Dawn. *Taliaferro*. Bloomington: Indiana University Press, 2007.

Leavitt, Bob. "Illini Take on Indiana Saturday." *Decatur Daily Review*, October 6, 1967.

McGee, Mac. "Fumbles Blunt Illini as Hoosiers Win 20-7 in Big Ten Opener." *Decatur Daily Review*, October 8, 1967.

McKesson, Jon. "Rose Rage Runs Rooters Ragged." *Indianapolis Star*, November 26, 1967.

McCawley, Harry. "Bowl Trip Beats Band Camp." *Republic* (Indiana), December 29, 1967.

McCawley, Harry. "TV (Sob) Disappoints John." *Republic* (Indiana), December 30, 1967.

"Many Techniques Used in Constructing Floats." *Indianapolis Star*, December 24, 1967.

Markus. "Harry and Jade: A Study of 2 Hoosiers." *Chicago Tribune*, October 28, 1967.

Marquette, Ray. "I.U. Shaves Kentucky." *Indianapolis Star*, September 24, 1967.

Marquette, Ray. "Pont Well Pleased with Soph Backs." *Indianapolis Star*, September 27, 1967.

Marquette, Ray. "Yippee! I.U. Nips Kansas, 18-15, Remains Unbeaten." *Indianapolis Star*, October 1, 1967.

Marquette, Ray. "Indiana Looking Like Bloomin' Winner." *Indianapolis Star*, October 2, 1967.

Marquette, Ray. "I.U. Uses New Script for 6th in Row." *Indianapolis Star*, October 29, 1967.

Marquette, Ray. "Perry Proves Capable in Relief of Gonso." *Indianapolis Star*, October 29. 1967.

Marquette, Ray. "Pont Feels Indiana Was Complete Team at Tucson." *Indianapolis Star*, October 30, 1967.

Marquette, Ray. "It's a Matter of Pride, No Miracle." *Indianapolis Star*, November 25, 1967.

Marquette, Ray. "Hoosiers Follow Same Script." *Indianapolis Star*, November 27, 1967.

Marquette, Ray. "Love Is a Thing Called Pont – I.U." *Indianapolis Star*, December 24, 1967.

Matthews, Dave. "Wolverines Challenge Perfect Indiana Record." *Lansing State Journal*, October 20, 1967.

Matthews, Dave. "Bump Proud of U-M Effort." *Lansing State Journal*, October 22, 1967.

Matthews, Dave. "Indiana Trips Skidding U-M." *Lansing State Journal*, October 22, 1967.

Miami University. "Cradle of Coaches: A Legacy of Excellence." Miami University Libraries, 2013. http://spec.lib.miamioh.edu//cradleofcoaches.

Moberg, McLain. "History of the Old Brass Spittoon." *USA Today Sports*, October 1, 2016. http://www.theonlycolors.com/2016/10/1/13117180/history-of-the-old-brass-spittoon-indiana-msu-michigan-state-rivalry.

Mooshil, Joe. "Indiana Heads 3 Contenders for Rose Bowl." *Post-Crescent* (Wisconsin), November 1, 1967.

Murphy, Bill. *The Cardiac Kids: A Season to Remember*. Bloomington, IN: Pen & Publish, 2007.

Murray, Jim. "Gambling Hoosiers Played their Hand to the End." *Los Angeles Times*, January 2, 1968.

Nelson, Murry. "The Illinois Slush Fund Scandal of 1966–67." October 20, 2014. https://ussporthistory.com/2014/10/20/the-illinois-slush-fund-scandal-of-1966-67.

Nims, Ernie. "Kazzie Gets His Man – Or You." *Bloomington Tribune*, November 16, 1967.

Nozell, John D. "Head of School Welcome." Cheshire Academy 1794. www.cheshireacademy.org.

Orwig, J. W. "Bill," Obituary from Kerley & Starks Funeral Homes, Inc., July 30, 1994.

Overpeck, Dave. "I.U. Thriller Act Comes Through Right on Time." *Indianapolis Star*, November 5, 1967.

Owens, Bob. "I.U. Chases Gophers in Run-for-the-Roses Bowl Bid Bait for Hoosiers." *Star-Tribune* (Minneapolis), November 17, 1967.

Parseghian, Ara. "Add Indiana to the List of November Surprises." *Indianapolis Star*, November 10, 1967.

"Plan Trip Well, Smith Warns Students." *Indiana Daily Student*, December 20, 1967.

"Plans Finalized for Bowl Tour." *Indiana Daily Student*, November 26, 1967.

"Poll-itis Has Meaning." *Indiana Daily Student*, November 1, 1967.

"Pont Polishes I.U. Defense for Kansas." *Indianapolis Star*, September 28, 1967.

"Pont Isn't Tossing In the Towel." *St. Cloud Times*, November 10, 1967.

"Pont's Relaxed Mien Surprises." *Indianapolis Star*, December 27, 1967.

Porter, Carl. "Lots of Crow to Eat." *Tucson Daily Citizen*, October 30, 1967.

Price, Nelson. *Indiana Legends: Famous Hoosiers from Johnny Appleseed to David Letterman.* Cincinnati, OH: Emmis Books, 2005.

Rager, Ann. "Indiana's New Band Director: Frederick C. Ebbs." I.U. News Bureau, p. 67.

Reed, Billy. "Our Half Is Coming Up, Said Bradshaw with 10-0 Lead." *Courier-Journal* (Louisville), September 24, 1967.

"Rose Bowl Heads List of I.U. Winter Sports." *Indiana Daily Student*, December 20, 1967.

"Rose Bowl Bound Hoosiers to Start Drills Wednesday." *Herald-Times* (Indiana), December 8, 1967.

Roth, Rick. "The Roth Report." *Indiana Daily Student*, November 17, 1967.

Roth, Rick. "I.U. Seeks 9th Victory at Minneapolis Today." *Indiana Daily Student*, November 18, 1967.

Roth, Rick. "Westward Ho! Indiana Ties for Big Ten Title, and Now, Baby, the Surf Is Up." *Indiana Daily Student*, November 28, 1967.

Roth, Rick. "It's 'I'm a Believer' as I.U. Heads for Roses; Stahr and Students Congratulate Footballers." *Indiana Daily Student*, November 28, 1967.

Roth, Rick. "I.U. Old Gray Mare in 1966; Thoroughbred Champion in 1967." *Indiana Daily Student*, December 1, 1967.

Roth, Rick, "Top-Ranked USC Trojans Shake Hoosiers' Rosy Dream." *Indiana Daily Student*, January 4, 1968.

Roth, Rick. "The Roth Report." *Indiana Daily Student*, January 6, 1968.

Salvani, Mady. "Red Blaik – A Football Giant." Army Athletic Communications, October 5, 2011.

Schneider, Jack. "IU's Gage 'Just Hugged' That Winning TD Pass." *Courier-Journal* (Louisville), September 24, 1967.

Senzell, Howard. East Coast Reacts to Hoosiers." *Indiana Daily Student*, November 16, 1967.

Smith, George. "We Weren't No. 3 Today,' Says Sad Jack." *Herald-Times* (Indiana), November 26, 1967.

"Sorry, Bowl Tickets Gone." *Herald-Times* (Indiana), November 20, 1967.

Special to the H-T. "World's Greatest College Weekend." *Herald-Times* (Indiana), April 24, 1998.

Special Correspondent. "Pont Picks 4 Yale Aides to Tutor Hoosiers." *Indianapolis Star*, January 29, 1965.

Spriggs, Dave. "Pont Holds Hoosiers in his Hands." *Tucson Daily Citizen*, October 30, 1967.

Stahr, Elvis J. Remarks at Big Ten Dinner Party, Hollywood Palladium, December 29, 1967.

Stahr, Elvis J. Kick-off Luncheon (Kiwanis), Pasadena Civic Auditorium, December 29, 1967.

"Stavroff Named I.U.'s Grid Captain, MVP." *Indianapolis Star*, November 23, 1966.

Sterling, Thayne. "Gage 'Grooves with Aretha.'" *Indiana Daily Student*, December 1, 1967.

Stowell, John. "Hoosiers Halt J-Hawks, 18-15." *Salina Journal*, October 1, 1967.

Stultz, Max. "It's Been a Long, Long Time: Indiana Wins Third Straight." *Indianapolis Star*, October 8, 1967.

Stultz, Max. "Pont's 'First' Is Memorable." *Indianapolis Star*, October 9, 1967.

Stultz, Max. "Hoosiers Pull Flim-Flam Job on Hawkeyes." *Indianapolis Star*, October 15, 1967.

Stultz, Max. "Hoosiers Get Away with One." *Indianapolis Star*, October 16, 1967.

Stultz, Max. "Between Games." *Indianapolis Star*, October 19, 1967.

Stultz, Max. "I.U. Underdog Again? Good." *Indianapolis Star*, November 1, 1967.

Stultz, Max. "Hoosiers Pass Omaha as MSU Falls." *Indianapolis Star*, November 12, 1967.

Stultz, Max. "I.U. Underdog Again? Good." *Indianapolis Star* (Indiana), November 13, 1967.

Stultz, Max. "To Err Human – Also Fatal for I.U." *Indianapolis Star*, November 19, 1967.

Stultz, Max. "I.U.'s Youngsters Lose with a Flair, Too." *Indianapolis Star*, November 20, 1967.

Stultz, Max. "More Roses for Pont: Coach of Year." *Indianapolis Star*, December 6, 1967.

Stultz, Max. "Cool California Weather Pleases." *Indianapolis Star*, December 22, 1967.

Stultz, Max. "Between Games." *Indianapolis Star*, December 29, 1967.

Sylvester, Curt. "Easy No. 2?—Hardly for U-M." *Detroit Free Press*, October 20, 1967.

Sylvester, Curt. "Sophs 'In' for U-M." *Detroit Free Press*, October 21, 1967.

Sylvester, Curt. "Hoosiers Win, 27-20." *Detroit Free Press*, October 22, 1967.

Taylor, Jim. "Indiana Stuns Boilermakers." *Toledo Blade*, November 26, 1967.

"They'll Play Too in Bowl of Roses." *Republic* (Indiana), December 29, 1967.

"Trimmed-Down Hoosiers Shaping Up for Chase." *Indianapolis Star*, September 17, 1967.

Underwood, John. "He's Burning to be a Success." *Sports Illustrated*, September 20, 1971. http://www.si.com/vault/1971/09/20/612423/hes-burning-to-be-a-success.

UPI. "Pont's Gamble Pays Off." *Tucson Daily Citizen*, October 26, 1967.

Wallace, William N. "Sid Gillman, 91, Innovator of Passing Strategy in Football." *New York Times*, January 4, 2003.

Wells, Herman B. *Being Lucky Reminiscences and Reflections*. Bloomington: Indiana University Press, 2012.

Williams, Bob. "High-Lites." *Indianapolis Star*, November 6, 1966.

"Wisconsin Throws Scare into Indiana, but Loses." *Post-Crescent* (Wisconsin), November 5, 1967.

Wynkoop, Mary Ann. *Dissent in the Heartland*. Bloomington: Indiana University Press, 2002.

Zimmerman, Paul. "Indiana Leader a Real Rooter." *Los Angeles Times*, December 29, 1967.

INDEX

4-4 defense 27
10 Essential Principles of Entrepreneurship You Never Learned in School 217
19 Stars of Indiana—Exceptional Hoosier Men 217
19 Stars of Indiana—Exceptional Hoosier Women 217
50 Crossword Puzzles with Playful Narrations 217
"76 Trombones" 163

A

Abbott, Bobby 50
Academic All-American 68, 171
Adams, Mike 43
Adventures in Hoosier Land 162
African American 47, 68, 96, 169, 170.
Akron, OH 23
Alabama (University) (Crimson Tide) 40, 47
Ali, Muhammad (Clay, Cassius) 169
All-American honorable mention 14
All-American honors 2
All-Big Ten 2, 67, 171
All-Mid-American Conference 14
Alumni Holidays, Inc. 139
Andrean High School 57, 100, 116, 117
Annapolis, MD 20
Ann Arbor, MI 81, 86, 105
Apisa, Bob 106, 108
Applegate, Steve (Plug) 43, 78, 92, 127, 129, 130, 131, 132, 133, 161, 175

Archbishop Moeller High School 31
Ariail, Warren (The Iceman) 28, 43, 68, 69, 90, 116, 142, 160, 166, 188
Arizona (University) (Wildcats) 42, 88, 89, 90, 91, 92, 93, 94, 96, 101, 135
Armed Forces Network 125
Army of Occupation in Europe 5
"Auld Lang Syne" 163

B

"Back Home Again in Indiana" 163
Baker, Bob (Coach) 16, 43, 50, 51, 126
Ball State University 51
Baltimore Colts 171
Bansch, John 17, 29, 57, 93, 96, 115, 156, 180, 181, 182
Barnett, John V. 141
Battle, Mike 160, 161, 162
Baughman, Mike 43, 57, 59, 132, 156, 162, 175
Beaver County, PA 39
Beban, Gary 147
Beef Bowl 151, 156
Belcher, Jodi v
Bell and Howell projector 47
Bell, Sam 24
Benton Harbor High School 5
Bergman, Bill 43
Berry, Jack 82, 182
Best, Bob 64
Bethel AME Church 142
Big Eight Conference 53
bigotry 69, 169
Big Seven 6
Big Ten 1, 4, 5, 6, 9, 10, 12, 13, 15, 17, 20, 21, 23, 27, 33, 34, 35, 39, 51, 57, 59, 60, 61, 62, 65, 68, 71, 73, 75, 76, 82, 83, 87, 88, 89, 90, 92, 93, 94, 102, 105, 113, 114, 119, 120, 121, 124, 125, 126, 127, 128, 135, 144, 147, 155, 169, 170, 171, 172, 179, 180, 187, 189, 192, 193
Big Ten Club of Southern California 153
Billingsley, Hobie 6
Bilunas, Tom 43, 100, 116, 160, 162, 165, 175
Blaik, Earl 15
Blanchard River 31
Bloomington, IN i, iii, iv, 5, 10, 19, 23, 34, 37, 38, 40, 46, 72, 89, 97, 101, 107, 114, 123, 124, 125, 128, 140, 141, 142, 170, 171, 175, 176, 179, 183, 187, 189, 190, 195
Bloomington Herald-Record 127
Bloomington Herald-Telephone 90
Bloomington High School 23

Index

Bloomington Kiwanis Club 9
Bloomington Tribune 90, 191
Bloomington Varsity Club 9
Bluebonnet Bowl 53
Board of Trustees 8, 169
Bomba, Brad (Dr.) 68, 96, 97, 107, 114, 126.
Borders, John 100
Bordner, Bill 43
Bowen, Governor 171
Boyajian, John 100, 101
Bozicevich, Dick 43
Brademas, John 20
Bradshaw, Charlie (Coach) 46, 47, 48, 49, 51, 192
Bragg, H.W. 151
Branigin, Roger D. 141
Braun, Howard 62
Brewer, Mel 62
Briscoe Quad 139
Broad Ripple High School 92
Brookside Park (Pasadena, CA) 152
Brown County State Park 1
Brown, Dennis 83, 84, 85, 88
Brown, Howard (Coach) (Gooner) 16, 21, 23, 24, 29, 36, 37, 38, 43, 116
Brownstown, IN (Jackson County Fair) 40
Bryan, Drew v
Bryant, Paul (Coach) (Bear) 40, 47
Buffalo Bills 172
Bumb, Jane 96
Butcher, Jade 23, 26, 43, 49, 51, 56, 64, 72, 73, 75, 79, 83, 84, 85, 91, 92, 93, 98, 109, 116, 117, 118, 120, 127, 129, 130, 155, 161, 164, 165, 167, 175, 180

C

Campbell, Eldon 141
Can Can 163
Canarecci, Frank 43
Canham, Don 81
Canton, OH 3
Canyon Inn 45, 54, 127
Cardiac Kids i, 72, 188, 190
Carlson, John 43
Carmichael, Hoagy 153, 154, 162
Carmichael, John 134
Caruthers, Ed 89

Cassells, Gary 39, 43, 57, 58, 65, 72, 73, 78, 90, 93, 120, 126, 127, 129, 140, 186
Chaffee, Roger 19
Chamberlain, Charles 115, 182, 183
Chambers of Commerce 15
Champaign-Urbana, IL 60, 61, 62, 63
Cheshire Academy 18, 191
Chicago Bears 53
Chicago Daily News 134
Chicago Football Writers 86
Chicago Tribune 90, 184, 189
Chiz, Bill 43
Christman, Paul 158
Christmas Day 152, 153
Christmas Eve 152
Cincinnati, OH 31, 35, 58, 127, 175, 192
Cincinnati (University) (Bearcats) 35
Cinderella Ball i, ii, vi, 12, 77, 78, 79
City College of San Francisco 148
Civil Rights Act 169
Civil War 31
Clark, George Rogers 86
Clemson (University) (Tigers) 15
Coach of the Year 111, 138, 142, 143
Cole, Terry (T-Bear) 17, 19, 36, 43, 47, 56, 57, 76, 79, 85, 86, 91, 109, 127, 129, 130, 131, 133, 153, 155, 161, 163, 164, 171, 172, 176, 180
Cole up the middle 127, 129
College Football Hall of Fame 22
Collins, Bob 50, 51, 72, 75, 82, 85, 86, 89, 119, 124, 133, 143, 144, 183, 184
Colosseum in Rome 8
Columbus, OH 33, 59, 89
Combes, Harry 62
Conard High School 58
Connecticut (state of) iv, 18, 58, 175
Cook, Bradley v
Counsilman, Doc 6, 7
Courier-Journal 90, 182, 185, 189, 192
Cream and Crimson 29, 46, 154
Crest toothpaste 11, 137
Crisler, Fritz 5, 6
Criter, Ken 95, 102
Crosby, Bing 124
Crusan, Doug (Monessen Monster) vi, 17, 18, 19, 24, 25, 26, 27, 38, 39, 43, 46, 47, 48, 60, 66, 67, 84, 87, 107, 108, 117, 119, 120, 129, 138, 158, 160, 171, 175, 181, 186

Index

Cunningham, Nate 27, 37, 43, 46, 47, 50, 66, 84, 91, 109, 110, 116, 159, 161, 162, 172, 175
Cuyahoga Falls High School 23

D

Dad's Day 72
Dallas Cowboys 172
Daniels, Mitch (Governor) iii, 171, 217
Danville, IL 37, 66, 175
Dartmouth (College) 97, 102
Daugherty, Duffy (Coach) 33, 34, 104, 105, 110, 128
David, John 43
Day, Ashley v
Dead Sea Scrolls 75
Deal, Mark v
Deal, Mike 43, 92, 163
Decatur, IL 108
DeGiacomo, Ken 19
DeMarco, Tom 43, 143
DeSalle, Don 43
Detroit Free Press 82, 182, 194
Detroit Lions 23
Detroit Tigers 32
Dickens, Phil (Coach) 2, 3, 6, 7, 8, 9, 10, 15, 20, 37, 137
Dirksen, Everett McKinley (Senator) 155, 157
Disneyland 152, 153, 159
Division I 14, 19, 20, 31, 35, 41, 59
Domres, Tom 95
Doninger, Clarence v, 175
Donnelly, Joe (Senator) ii
Dortch, Carl R. 141
Douglass, Bobby 43, 54, 56, 57
Duffy, Kevin vi, 17, 27, 28, 43, 54, 67, 71, 95, 96, 100, 101, 106, 107, 110, 111, 132, 164
Dumke, Mike 43
Dunn, Harold 43

E

East Lansing, MI 35, 102, 103, 106, 112
East Saint Louis Senior High 36
Ebbs, Frederick C. (Professor) 139, 192
Ed Sullivan Show 59
Egan, Pat 43
Elkhart, IN 163

Elliott, Pete (Coach) (Bump) 62, 83, 86
Elyria, OH 32
Enderly, Dick 119
Eva Gordon High School 38
Evans, Dave 43, 143, 172

F

Faculty Committee on Athletics (IU) 8
Fairfield, Herb (Coach) 15, 43, 126
fiftieth anniversary iv
Fighting Hoosiers 138
Findlay High School 31
Findlay, OH (Flag City USA) 31, 33, 49, 175
Flag City USA 31
Flim-Flam Job 75, 193
Florida (University) (Gators) 28
Ford, Gerald R. 5, 22
Fort Wayne, IN 90, 99
Fort Wayne Journal-Gazette 90
Fostoria, OH 32
four-point stance 26
Frankenstein 152
Friedlander, Zeke 147
Fry, Jay (Coach) 15, 43

G

Gage, Al 26, 36, 37, 43, 49, 50, 51, 56, 67, 85, 99, 108, 117, 120, 158, 161, 163, 164, 165, 167, 175, 192, 193
Game of the Century 103
Gann, Roger 46
Gary, IN iv, 22, 57, 100, 116, 117, 175, 177
Gatorade 28, 90
Geers, Bob 43
Ghrist, Don 43
Gill, Cordell 17, 20, 42, 43, 63, 67, 107, 175
Gillman, Sid 15, 195
goblins 95
Go for fifty! Go for fifty! 92
Gonso, Harry (Baby Bull) iii, 29, 31, 32, 33, 34, 35, 36, 38, 41, 43, 46, 48, 49, 50, 51, 52, 55, 56, 57, 58, 64, 65, 67, 69, 72, 73, 74, 75, 77, 78, 84, 85, 86, 91, 96, 97, 98, 99, 100, 101, 107, 108, 109, 111, 114, 115, 116, 117, 118, 119, 120, 126, 127, 128, 129, 130, 146, 156, 158, 159, 160, 161, 163, 164, 165, 167, 171, 175, 180, 183, 185, 190
Gowdy, Curt 158

Index

Grady, Al 75, 185
Graham, Otto 20
Gray, Russell 123
Grecco, Jerry 43, 66, 100, 117, 159, 165
Green Bay Packers 41
Greene, Lorne 155
Griese, Bob 114, 126
Grissom, Virgil (Gus) 19
Grover, Roger 43
Grow, Red 43, 166
Gruber, Steve 43
Gunn, Jim 164

H

Hackney, Carol Cole v, 19
Hadl, John 53
Haglund, Mary Lynn (Miss Indiana) 155, 157
"Hail to the Victors" 82, 84
Halloween 95, 96
Hamelin, Joe 110
Hammond Clark High School 38
Hammond, IN 38, 176
Handley, Harold W. 141, 153, 187
Hanratty, Terry 22, 147
Hansel and Gretel 118
Harmon, Tom 22, 166
Harms, Fritz 61, 65
Harrison, Ed 43
Hayes, Woody (Coach) 3, 14, 15, 33, 35, 59, 63, 185
Hayhoe, Mike 163
Heaton, John 18
Heisman Trophy 20, 22, 147, 166
Helms Athletic Foundation 165
Henry, David 62
Heritage Woods Road 59
"He's got the Rose Bowl in his hands" 93
"He's got the whole world in His hands" 41, 42
Hickman, KY 46
Hicks, Bob (Coach) 7, 16, 43
Hoehn, Dave 43
Hoerner, Bob 82, 105, 110, 187, 188
homecoming patsy 97
Hooker, John 142, 168
Hoosier Group 1
Hope, Bob 29, 140

203

Horace Mann High School 22
Houston Oilers 172
Huff, Bill 43
Hula Bowl 120, 166
human sexual behavior 10
Huntington-Sheraton Hotel (LA, CA) 151

I

IBJ (Indianapolis Business Journal) ii, v, 217
IBJ Book Publishing, LLC v
Ice Miller 171
Idaho State (University) (Tigers) 20
I formation 24, 25
Illinois State (University) (Illini) iv, 42, 60, 61, 62, 63, 64, 65, 66, 67, 100, 110, 135, 189, 191
Indiana (University) (IU) (Hoosiers) i, ii, v, vi, 1, 2, 3, 4, 5, 6, 7, 8, 9, 10, 11, 12, 13, 15, 16, 17, 18, 19, 20, 21, 22, 23, 24, 33, 34, 35, 36, 37, 39, 40, 41, 42, 45, 46, 47, 48, 49, 50, 51, 53, 54, 56, 57, 58, 59, 60, 61, 62, 63, 64, 65, 66, 68, 71, 72, 73, 74, 75, 79, 81, 82, 83, 84, 85, 86, 87, 88, 89, 90, 91, 92, 93, 94, 96, 97, 98, 99, 100, 101, 102, 103, 104, 105, 106, 107, 108, 109, 110, 111, 114, 115, 116, 117, 118, 119, 120, 121, 123, 124, 125, 126, 128, 129, 130, 132, 133, 134, 135, 137, 138, 139, 140, 141, 142, 144, 145, 146, 147, 148, 151, 152, 153, 154, 155, 156, 157, 158, 159, 160, 161, 162, 163, 164, 165, 167, 168, 169, 170, 171, 172, 175, 176, 179, 180, 181, 182, 183, 184, 185, 186, 187, 188, 189, 190, 191, 192, 193, 194, 195
Indiana Daily Student 3, 49, 140, 168, 179, 182, 184, 185, 186, 187, 188, 191, 192, 193
"Indiana, Our Indiana" 163
Indianapolis, IN ii, iv, v, 17, 19, 21, 28, 51, 56, 57, 59, 63, 65, 86, 90, 92, 93, 105, 110, 113, 114, 115, 119, 124, 133, 144, 146, 147, 156, 160, 163, 176, 179, 180, 181, 182, 183, 184, 185, 186, 188, 189, 190, 191, 193, 194, 195, 198
Indianapolis 500 Memorial Day auto classic 163
Indianapolis News 90
Indianapolis Star v, 17, 51, 56, 57, 59, 65, 86, 90, 93, 105, 110, 114, 115, 119, 124, 133, 144, 147, 156, 160, 176, 179, 180, 181, 182, 183, 184, 185, 186, 188, 189, 190, 191, 193, 194, 195
Indiana University archives v, 14, 25, 32, 43, 48, 55, 58, 77, 78, 79, 99, 131, 135, 143, 156, 157
Indiana University Hall of Fame 171
Indiana University Medical School 168
Indiana University School of Law i, 171
Indiana University Student Foundation 11

Index

Iowa (University) (Hawkeyes) 13, 17, 42, 69, 71, 72, 73, 74, 75, 76, 83, 135, 139, 169, 185, 193
Iowa City Press-Citizen 75
Iowa Hawkeye Marching Band 139
I-Pro-screen 72, 73
I-Pro-screen-left 72
Isenbarger, John (Iso) 21, 22, 25, 29, 35, 38, 43, 49, 50, 51, 55, 56, 64, 65, 66, 73, 74, 76, 77, 83, 84, 85, 86, 87, 91, 94, 97, 98, 100, 101, 108, 109, 110, 114, 116, 117, 127, 128, 129, 130, 132, 139, 146, 156, 157, 158, 159, 160, 162, 163, 166, 167, 171, 176, 180, 186
It's Midnight, Cinderella 165
IU Fight Song 155
IU Marching Hundred 139, 155, 162
IU physical education center 17
IU Press v
IU Student Rose Bowl Committee 138
Ivory soap commercial 124

J

Jenkins, Dan 97, 99, 101, 104, 189
Jimmy the Greek 147
Johnson, Rich 61
Johnson, Ron 82, 84, 85, 88, 162
Jones, Dr. Clarence 123
Jordan, Leroy 40
Journal of Dental Research 11
Journal of the American Dental Association 11
Jurkiewicz, Walter 43
Just punt the damn ball 84

K

Kaczmarek, Ken (Kenny) (Kaz) iii, vi, 17, 19, 20, 27, 28, 39, 43, 61, 66, 67, 84, 85, 95, 101, 102, 106, 107, 108, 110, 117, 119, 120, 132, 133, 152, 159, 162, 166, 172, 176, 189
Kamradt, Al 43
Kamzelski, Ron 117
Kansas City, MO 41
Kansas State (University) 13, 19, 36
Kansas (University) (Jayhawks) 13, 19, 36, 41, 42, 52, 53, 54, 56, 57, 61, 63, 65, 67, 77, 100, 135, 166, 187, 190, 191
Keiffner, Pat v
Kellams, Dina v
Kentucky (University) (Wildcats) 21, 24, 36, 42, 45, 46, 47, 48, 49, 50, 51, 54, 60, 61, 63, 67, 100, 125, 135, 189

Keyes, Leroy (Amazing Mr. Everything) 114, 125, 126, 130, 134, 162
Kinsey Institute 10, 11, 89, 137, 183, 189
Kinsey Report 89
Kirk, Bob 26, 27, 43, 114, 142, 143, 152, 167
Kirk Sr., Rev. Robert 142
Kiss me, I'm a Hoosier 146
Kiwanians 15
Kleinschmidt, Dean v, 40, 41, 42, 68, 176
knothole kids 97
Knox, Elyse 22
Kornowa, Dave 37, 38, 43, 50, 56, 57, 64, 68, 86, 90, 92, 108, 110, 117, 129, 131, 158, 159, 161, 162, 166, 176, 187
Kristen (Hambridge) Draskovic v
Krivoshia, Mike 39, 43, 51, 73, 78, 85, 100, 108, 110, 129, 161, 172

L

Lancaster High School 59
Lansing State Journal 82, 105, 110, 184, 187, 188, 190
Lawry's Prime Rib in Beverly Hills 151
Leahy, Frank (Coach) 47
Lee, Dwight 106
Lesch, Millard v
Levy, Morris (Blondie) v, 29, 36, 39, 43, 68, 92, 176.
Lexington, KY 46
Libbey High School 5
Little 500 11, 29
Loftman, Guy 138
Long, Bob 43
Long, Ken 43
Louisville (University) (Cardinals) 18
Los Angeles, CA 22, 116, 145, 146, 147, 151, 152, 162, 183, 185, 188, 191, 195
Los Angeles Rams 22
Lyons, Dicky 46

M

Mackey, Red 134
Madison Heights High School 51
Madison, James v
Magner, Gary 165
Magnolia, MS 38
Make Your Pasadena Reservations Now 112
Malinchak, Bill 19
Manitowoc Herald-Times 115, 183

Index

Mansfield, OH 32, 58
Mansfield High School 58
Marion, OH 32
Marks, Brown 27, 28, 38, 43, 62, 65, 71, 74, 95, 96, 100, 132, 152
Marquette, Ray 56, 59, 64
Mathias, Jay 43, 92, 156
Matishak, John 93
Maurer, Janie vi, 217
Maurer, Michael S. (Mickey) i, ii, 217
Mauro, Harold (Monk) 17, 39, 40, 43, 57, 65, 72, 73, 98, 119, 126, 127, 132, 161, 164, 172, 176
McCaa, Bill 43
McConnell, Robert B. 141
McCormick, John 45
McCormick's Creek State Park 45, 54, 71, 126
McCullouch, Earl 159
McDaniel, Charlie (Coach) 16
McDermott, Eugene 105
McKay, John (Coach) 104, 147
McKesson, John 133
McMillin, Bo (Coach) 3, 23
Memorial Stadium 1, 36, 46, 61, 72, 97, 123, 125, 139, 172
Merchant Marine Academy 20
Miami Dolphins 171
Miami (University) (Miami of Ohio) 3, 13, 15, 24, 27, 35, 40, 126, 190
Michigan (University) (Wolverines) 2, 5, 16, 20, 21, 22, 23, 33, 34, 35, 39, 40, 42, 76, 81, 82, 83, 84, 85, 86, 87, 89, 90, 100, 101, 102, 103, 104, 105, 106, 107, 108, 109, 110, 111, 114, 124, 125, 128, 135, 137, 139, 162, 166, 169, 171, 183
Michigan athletic director 81
Michigan State (University) (Spartans) (Sparty) 16, 21, 23, 33, 34, 35, 40, 42, 82, 83, 101, 102, 103, 104, 105, 106, 107, 108, 109, 110, 111, 114, 125, 128, 135, 139, 166, 169, 182, 183
Michigan State University of Agriculture and Applied Science 103
Midland High School 39
Midwest Back of the Week 133
Midwest Coach of the Week 133
Midwest Lineman of the Week 87, 93, 133
Mills, Doug 62
Minnesota (University) (Golden Gophers) 16, 26, 42, 83, 89, 104, 105, 111, 112, 113, 114, 115, 116, 117, 118, 119, 120, 124, 125, 126, 127, 128, 134, 135, 139, 148, 176
Mitchell, Fred 43
Mitchell, IN iv, 19, 43
Mitchell High School 19

Mollenkopf, Jack (Coach) (Fat Jack) (the Ripper) 4, 63, 125, 134, 144, 147
Monessen, PA 18, 175
Moore, Steve 43
Moore, Wally (Coach) 20
morphine 68
Mourouzis, Nick (Coach) v, 16, 27, 33, 43, 64, 74, 126, 176
Moynihan, Bob 38, 43, 62, 160, 162, 166, 176
Mudra, Darrell (Coach) 90, 91, 93
Muhler, Joseph Charles 11
Muncie, IN iv, 21, 22, 128, 157, 176, 183
Muncie Central High School 21
Murphy, Audie 156
Murphy, Charlie 43

N

Najam, Ted 170
Namath, Joe 40
Naponic, Bob 61, 64
National Academy 11
National Football Writers Association 140, 142
National Football Writers Association All-American team 140
National Guardsmen 115
Naval Academy 20
NCAA 2, 6, 7, 9, 10, 138, 142, 170
NCAA probation 6, 10
NCAA rules 2, 142
Nebergall, William H. 11
Nebraska (University) (Cornhuskers) 6, 12, 36
New Year's Day 4, 113, 138
New York Times 10, 185, 195, 217
NFL 22, 23, 26, 41, 105, 171
Nichols, Bob 43, 160
Nichols, Gary 43
Nichols, Nichelle (Uhura) 71
Nick's 101, 134
"Night and Day" 163
Nitschke, Ray 41
Nobel Laureate 11
Norman, Ben (Benny) 43, 64, 72, 170
North Carolina State (University) (Wolfpack) 97
North Carolina (University) (Tarheels) 24, 97
Northwestern (University) (Wildcats) 3, 14, 20, 24, 169, 170
Notre Dame (University) (Fighting Irish) 3, 4, 19, 20, 22, 33, 35, 47, 72, 103, 104, 105, 125, 147, 163

Index

Novocain 68
Nowatzke, Tom 93

O

Ohio Lineman of the Year 59
Ohio State (University) (Buckeyes) 15, 16, 20, 21, 22, 23, 27, 31, 35, 39, 59, 63, 88, 89, 93, 124, 172
Oklahoma (University) (Sooners) 53
Old Oaken Bucket 4, 123, 139, 171
O'Leary, Helene v
Olssen, Lance 127
Ontario, CA 146
"On the Banks of the Wabash" 46
Oregon (University) (Ducks) 6
Orr, Governor 171
Orwig, James Wilfred (Bill) 1, 2, 3, 5, 6, 9, 10, 11, 12, 13, 16, 17, 29, 46, 59, 60, 75, 81, 86, 97, 114, 125, 128, 134, 137, 141, 144, 168, 170, 171, 176, 187, 191
Orwig, Jane 59, 75, 81
Orwig, Jr., J. W. (Bill) v, 81, 176
Overpeck, Dave 101
Owens, Jessie 22
Oxford University (England) 12

P

Pac-8 105, 113, 147, 149
Pacific Coast Conference 105
Pankratz, Karl vi, 34, 35, 36, 41, 43, 49, 64, 67, 90, 152, 159, 162, 176
Parmelee, Mickey 17
Parseghian, Ara (Coach) 3, 14, 15, 22, 104, 105, 191
Pasadena, CA ii, 4, 112, 114, 124, 125, 134, 137, 138, 139, 141, 146, 151, 153, 155, 167, 169, 193
"Pasadena A-Go-Go" 125
Passionate Father's Retreat 155
Paul, Hal 33
Paulus, Bill 43
Pennsylvania State (University) (Penn State) (Nittany Lion) 18, 39
Perry, Mike (Redbird) 29, 36, 43, 73, 78, 91, 92, 93, 94, 96, 100, 101, 126, 132, 164, 176, 190.
Peterson, Al 38
Petra, Edwin G. 146
Phipps, Mike 114, 126, 128
Piccolo, Brian ("Brian's Song") 53
Pittsburgh (University) (Panthers) 6

Plank, Ernie (Coach) 15, 27, 43, 126, 159
Podolak, Ed 73
Pont, John (Coach) ii, 3, 4, 5, 12, 13, 14, 15, 16, 17, 20, 21, 23, 24, 25, 26,
   27, 28, 29, 34, 35, 36, 37, 38, 39, 40, 41, 43, 45, 46, 47, 50, 51, 56, 59,
   60, 62, 63, 64, 65, 66, 67, 69, 73, 74, 75, 76, 83, 84, 85, 86, 87, 88, 89,
   90, 91, 92, 93, 94, 95, 96, 97, 98, 102, 103, 104, 106, 109, 110, 111,
   112, 113, 114, 115, 116, 117, 118, 119, 120, 126, 127, 128, 129, 130,
   132, 133, 134, 138, 139, 140, 142, 143, 145, 146, 147, 151, 152, 154,
   155, 159, 160, 161, 165, 166, 167, 168, 169, 170, 172, 179, 180, 181,
   182, 184, 185, 186, 188, 189, 190, 191, 193, 194
Porter, Cole 153, 163
Price, Clarence 21, 43, 63, 100, 170
Pro Football Hall of Fame 3
"Punt John Punt" 98
Purdue (University) (Boilermakers) 3, 4, 13, 16, 20, 23, 33, 40, 42, 63, 78,
   89, 92, 105, 111, 112, 114, 115, 118, 119, 120, 123, 124, 125, 126,
   127, 128, 129, 130, 131, 132, 133, 134, 135, 137, 138, 139, 140, 141,
   144, 147, 163, 172, 181, 182, 183, 186, 194

R

Rabold, John 43
Raye, Jimmy 106
Red Cedar River 103
Reddick, Mel 98, 101
Reed, Marc 91
Rhodes scholarship 12
Rhodus, Doug 43
Rice, Doug 35
Riggins, Junior 54
Robinson, Gayle 43
Rodgers, "Pepper" (Coach) 54, 57
Roederer, Susan vi
Rookie of the Year 171
Roosevelt High School 63
Rose Bowl i, ii, 3, 5, 22, 24, 37, 38, 42, 62, 63, 82, 93, 104, 105, 111, 112,
   113, 114, 115, 116, 119, 121, 124, 128, 134, 135, 137, 138, 139, 141,
   142, 144, 145, 146, 147, 151, 152, 153, 155, 156, 157, 158, 161, 163,
   164, 165, 166, 167, 168, 169, 172, 176, 179, 185, 187, 188, 190, 192
Rose Bowl Float Fund Committee 141
Rose Bowl kickoff banquet 142
Rose Bowl Parade 139, 155
Rosolina, Rachel v
Rossovich, Tim (Timbo) 147, 148, 158, 159
Rotarians 15
Roth, Mike 43

Index

Roth, Rick 49, 168, 192
Runyon, Ashley v
Rupp, Adolph 21
Russell, Bob (Bull) 17, 39, 43, 57, 58, 65, 69, 71, 72, 78, 83, 119, 123, 126, 127, 131, 167, 168, 179, 186
Ryun, Jim 57

S

Sagamore of the Wabash 171
Saint Augustine 20
Saint Francis de Sales 34
San Diego Chargers 172
San Francisco Youth Guidance Center 148
San Gabriel Mountains 155
Santa Claus 144
Sayers, Gale 53
Schleuter, Doug 92
Schmidt, Al 43, 92, 143
Scott High School 5
Senior Bowl 120
Sexual Behavior in the Human Female 10
Sexual Behavior in the Human Male 10
Shanklin, Donnie 54
Shine, Tom v
Shortridge High School 21, 63
Sigma Alpha Epsilon 36
Simic, Curt 168
Simon, Bill 43
Simpson, O.J. (Juice) 126, 134, 140, 148, 152, 159, 160, 161, 162, 163, 164, 165, 181, 185
Singing Hoosiers 153, 154, 155, 185, 188
Skyline Conference 2
slush fund 62
Smith, Bubba 16, 35
Smith, Herbert 139
Smothers Brothers 153
Smulyan, Jeff v, 147
Sniadecki, Jim 27, 43, 71, 133, 138, 172
Snowden, Cal vi, 43, 48, 63, 68, 129, 132, 156, 172
Sousa, John Philip 82
South Bend, IN iv, 58, 176, 177
South Bend Riley High School 58
South Carolina (state of) 68
Spartan Stadium 103, 104
Spickard, Rick 17, 39, 43, 64

Sports Illustrated 8, 28, 97, 99, 104, 148, 189, 194
Spriggs, Dave 92
Stahr Jr., Elvis Jacob (President) (Colonel) 12, 46, 137, 140, 141, 144, 153, 154, 157, 165, 167, 168, 192, 193
Stanford (University) (Tree) 54
"Stardust" 154, 162
Starr, Bart 41
Star Trek 71
Star Trek Command 71
Staubach, Roger 20
Stavroff, Frank 15, 17, 21, 24, 37, 39, 106, 193
St. Cloud Times 118, 119, 128, 191
Steele, T.C. 1
St. John Arena 35
St. Joseph High School 19
St. Louis Cardinals 172
Stokely-Van Camp 28
Stolberg, Eric vi, 23, 24, 36, 43, 49, 50, 62, 84, 87, 108, 127, 129, 130, 132, 133, 160, 164, 167, 171, 172, 176, 179
stonecutter (cutter) 23
Strois, Sam 111
Strother, Linda (Queen) 151, 157
Stultz, Max 75, 110, 117, 119, 160
Super Bowl I 41

T

Tangerine Bowl 39
Tarawa 68
Tennessee State (University) (Tigers) 26
Terry P. Cole memorial scholarship 172
Texas Christian (University) (Horned Frog) 72
Thanksgiving Day 126
Thaxton, Greg 43
The Athletic Department 7
The Big Ten skywriters 17
The black boycott of 1969 170
The Buckeye Conference 32
The Cradle of Coaches 15
the Holy Ghost 50
The Old Brass Spittoon 105, 106
The Persian Warriors 148
"There are three things that can happen when you pass, ..." 15
The Region iv
The World's Greatest College Weekend 11

Index

Thornhill, Charlie 35
tie one for the Gipper 104
Toledo Blade 133, 194
Toledo, OH 5, 31, 34, 37, 176
Toledo (University) (Rockets) 5
Tournament of Roses Committee 152
Tournament of Roses Director's Dinner 153
training room abuses iv
Tuchman, Steve v, 138
Tucson Daily Citizen 90, 92, 184, 188, 191, 193, 194

U

UCLA (Bruins) 54, 97, 102, 116, 134, 147, 153, 155, 164
UCLA Basketball Classic 153, 155
UK Law School 46
Underground Railroad 31
United Press International Back of the Week 51
United States Army Air Corps 22
United States Army lieutenant colonel 12
United States secretary of the army 12
Universal Studios 152
University of Michigan Athletic Hall of Honor 171
University of Southern California (USC) (Trojans) v, 97, 104, 134, 138, 140, 147, 148
UPI coaches' poll 71
US Navy 14, 27
US Olympic track team 23
US Postal Service 103

V

Valek, Jim (Coach) 62
Vanoy, Vernon 54, 55
Van Schoyck, Jake (Coach) 15, 43
Varsity Club 9, 29
Verlihay, Ted 43
Verona, PA 39, 176
Veteran's Day, November 11 102
Vietnam War 63
Vincennes, IN 86
Virginia Tech (University) (HokieBird) 97, 102
Volkman, Dean 64, 65

W

WAC 94, 135
Waltz, Dick 43
Warmath, Murray (Coach) 120, 134, 180
Warner, Don (Donny) 43, 46, 49, 56, 57, 64, 66, 74, 83, 86, 91, 100, 116, 172, 177
Warriner, Tom 43
Washington, DC iv, 20, 63, 68, 175, 176
Washington State (University) (Cougars) 16
Water Colors 217
Watson, James 12
Weathersfield High School 18
Webster, George 35
Weir Cook Airport 113
Wells, Herman B (President) 7, 9, 10, 11, 12, 140, 145, 167, 182, 183, 195
We Shall Return 167
West Lafayette, IN 17, 23, 125, 128, 171
"We've Got the Whole World in Our Hands" 63
Wheeler, Sam 99
White, Betty 155
"White Christmas" 124
White, Ed 19
White, E. G. (Eugene) 43, 58
Whitehead, Julia v
Wilcox, Howdy 11
Wilkinson, Bud 53
Williams, John 119
Williams, Perry 126, 132
Willson, Meredith 163
Wilson, Cal 43
Wilson, Carl 119
Wilson, Kenneth (Big Ten commissioner) (Tug) 7, 9
Wintermute, John 119
Wisconsin (University) (Badgers) 42, 77, 94, 95, 96, 97, 98, 99, 100, 101, 102, 103, 104, 119, 124, 134, 135, 185, 195
Wolfe, Bill 43, 108, 143, 165
Woodworth, Samuel 123
World War II 12, 68, 156
Wortley, George 43
Wright, John 61, 66
Wyoming (University) (Cowboys) 2, 7, 19, 97

Index

Y

Yale (University) (Bulldogs) 3, 12, 15, 193
Yary, Ron 140, 148, 160, 161
Ye Olde Regulator 134
Young, Adrian 140, 147, 158
Youngman, Henny 92

ABOUT THE AUTHOR

Michael S. ("Mickey") Maurer's career as an attorney and entrepreneur has included cable television, film production, radio broadcasting, publishing, real estate and banking.

He serves as Chairman of the Board of IBJ Corporation and The National Bank of Indianapolis. He is a regular columnist for the *Indianapolis Business Journal* and a regular contributor to the *New York Times* crossword puzzle. He is author of *Water Colors: The Photographs of Michael S. Maurer, 19 Stars of Indiana: Exceptional Hoosier Women, 19 Stars of Indiana: Exceptional Hoosier Men, 10 Essential Principles of Entrepreneurship You Never Learned in School and 50 Crossword Puzzles with Playful Narrations.* He lives in Carmel, Indiana, with his wife, Janie. They have three children and nine grandchildren. Contact Maurer at: mmaurer@ibj.com.